GAME COOKERY

GAME
COOKERY

Angela Humphreys

David & Charles

Illustrations by John Paley

A DAVID & CHARLES BOOK

Copyright © Angela Humphreys 1986, 1993

First published 1986
Reprinted 1988
New edition 1993
First paperback edition 1997
Reprinted 1998

A catalogue record for this book is available from the British Library.

ISBN 0 7153 0721 5

Printed in Great Britain by Redwood Books, Trowbridge, Wiltshire
for David & Charles
Brunel House   Newton Abbot   Devon

14 95

CONTENTS

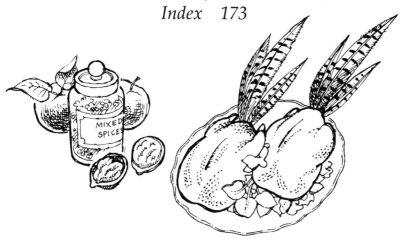

The author would like to thank *Sporting Gun* for their
kind permission to reproduce recipes which have
featured in this magazine

FOREWORD

Cookery writers would appear to breed faster than the proverbial rabbit. It would seem that there are more people giving cookery hints than actually sitting down at a table to eat. We live in a world full of experts, but sadly many are rather more expert at projecting themselves than they are in their chosen field.

It gives me special pleasure, therefore, to have the opportunity of shedding a little light on a very charming (not to mention attractive) someone who really does have something to offer.

Under the guise of Guidwife, Angela has been providing monthly recipes for *Sporting Gun*'s 'Sportsman's Kitchen' for nearly four years. In view of her continuing originality it is hardly surprising that she has built a keen following in shooting circles.

What is surprising is that Angela has had no formal training. Her inspiration has been an interest in cookery, combined with a good supply of game from the three hungry males who share her house. Their excellent condition offers the perfect advertisement for Angela's kitchen skills—the young boys are growing upward at a rate of knots, while hubbie John (a well-known sporting writer) fights a running battle against growth in a different direction.

We'll blame the latter dilemma on the ballast, for Angela has a keen and genuine interest in health and fitness, a fact reflected by her recipes. She quite rightly points out that game, fowl and fish offer some of the healthiest meats you could wish for.

You will find her dishes imaginative, inexpensive and with enough variety to suit all occasions. Moreover, they have all been given the ultimate seal of approval by the traditional method—her own dining table.

Rather than being another book from a well-known cook or actress simply lending her name to yet another assortment of casseroles and coq variations, this is the real thing. And for that there's no substitute.

MIKE BARNES
FORMER EDITOR, *Sporting Gun*

Grouse

ENTRÉE

The aims of this book are twofold. Firstly, for the housewife with shooting men and anglers in her family who regularly bring home an assortment of game for table or freezer. It can be a daunting prospect to deal with six brace of pheasant or a dozen pigeon, but any thrifty housewife, knowing the high price of meat, will feel obliged to make use of any meat which costs her nothing. She can be assured that it is full of flavour and free from the additives used by farmers to enhance the bulk and flavour of their meat.

Secondly, it is for those who have never cooked game before because they considered it too expensive, too highly flavoured or too difficult to prepare. Game need not be any of these; it is becoming more widely available to non-shooting families, either oven-ready from the supermarket or in feather or fur from the butcher or game dealer. Leading supermarket chains are now selling a wide variety of oven-ready game in season. Each pack is clearly labelled with the age, species and a suggested cooking method; leaflets with recipes are often available. Because this game is sold oven-ready and only the best quality is offered, this does mean that the price is of necessity higher than game bought unprepared from the butcher or game dealer. The fact that game no longer carries the old label of exclusiveness and is now gracing the table of a much wider section of the public can only be good news for shooting man, game dealer and consumer.

There are endless ways of cooking game; it is appropriate for everyday family meals, Sunday lunches, special occasions, for picnics or barbecues. Most experts would agree that young game which has been cleanly shot is best cooked plainly and simply; a young roasted bird takes some beating, but there are times when the game is old or badly shot when it calls for more careful cooking to do it justice. This is when you can experiment with different casseroles, pot-roasts, pies and soups, trying new combinations of ingredients to include vegetables, fruits, herbs and spices.

As game birds tend to dry out easily in the cooking, the French method of roasting is ideal for them. For this the birds are roasted covered, with stock or wine added, instead of the dry-roast method so popular in the United Kingdom. A 'self-basting' roasting tin produces a similar result and is ideal for pheasants and all the small game birds. A pressure cooker is an invaluable aid to the game cook for preparing a complete meal quickly; a rabbit stew, for example, may take as little as 25 minutes to cook, and the gravy will be rich and well flavoured. It is also useful for the initial cooking of a tough old hare or 'fork bender' cock pheasant. This will help to tenderise the meat before you begin to follow the recipe.

Occasionally the bag will contain only three-quarters of a badly shot or dogged bird, or you may be left with several legs after making a 'breast only' dish. These oddments should not be wasted but are ideal for use in pâtés, burgers, pies or soups.

Many modern families have barbecues in the garden, or enjoy cooking out of doors on an open fire. Provided that the meat is marinated beforehand and basted during cooking, or foil wrapped to keep it moist, game can make a delicious alternative to the traditional and boring beefburgers and sausages. Provided that they are young, joints of rabbit, grouse, pheasant or partridge can all be successfully barbecued.

In the past game cooking has been associated with the old farmhouse kitchen range, but kitchens today tend to be equipped with a variety of different types of cooker—gas, electric or the microwave oven. More and more microwave ovens are creeping into kitchens and their sales have rocketed over the past few years. In 1984, the Microwave Oven Association and Market Assessment forecast sales of 1,150,000 for 1986. However, for most families a microwave oven is complementary to the deep freeze and to their traditional oven rather than a substitute for it. It is useful if you are forgetful about removing food from the freezer for defrosting or if your family meals are at irregular times or endlessly interrupted, in which case food may either need to be cooked quickly from frozen or reheated. This equally applies to cooked game dishes as well as to other ready-cooked meals or convenience foods straight from the freezer. Game dishes can also be successfully prepared in the microwave, but it is better if the oven has facilities for browning and slow cooking. A roasted bird looks more appetising if served with a crisp golden-brown skin, and a good old-fashioned jugged hare needs long slow cooking both to tenderise the meat and to allow the full rich flavour to develop.

Entrée

If you follow the advice of most doctors and go for a low-fat diet, then game is ideal. There is very little natural fat on any game and any excess oiliness sometimes present in wildfowl drains off the birds if they are roasted on a trivet. Low in fat also means fewer calories and is therefore a valuable aid to those watching their waistlines and seeking variety to endless dishes of chicken and cottage cheese.

Whenever possible, I have tried to avoid the use of extra fat during cooking. It is not essential, for example, to fry meat in butter or oil before cooking it in a casserole. When roasting small game birds or venison, a little extra fat or bacon may be needed to prevent the meat from becoming dry, but this should always be skimmed off before making the gravy or sauce. Larger birds should be roasted breast down to ensure that the juices run into and not off the breast, thus helping to keep the meat moist. Instead of using the roux method of mixing butter and flour with milk for making sauces, try blending cornflour and skimmed milk. Some of the richer recipes include cream, but top of the milk, natural low-fat yoghurt or fromage frais may be substituted.

We are also encouraged to eat more fibre and less salt in our diet. This may be achieved by using puréed vegetables or wholemeal flour to thicken gravies and sauces, and by using only a little salt and adding herbs and spices for extra flavour.

As well as the traditional game companions of cranberry or redcurrant jelly, fried breadcrumbs or game chips, there are many other flavours which enhance and complement game. Red cabbage braised with onions, apples and vinegar, crunchy salads, apricots, apples, pears and pineapple all add different tastes and textures. Home-made elderberry, rowan or crab-apple jelly with their rich earthy flavours are just as agreeable as the shop-bought cranberry or redcurrant.

Whether you are an experienced game cook or a complete beginner, I hope you will take a chance, experiment and enjoy cooking and eating some of the dishes which follow.

Note: Quantities are given in metric and imperial measurements. Use one set only; never mix them as they are not exact equivalents.

Cooking times may vary slightly according to the type of oven used.

1

FIT FOR THE TABLE

A GUIDE TO THE PREPARATION OF GAME

In most shooting and fishing households it is the menfolk who have the pleasure of the day in the field and it seems to me only fair that they should also prepare the game they have brought home and present it ready for the oven to the sporting wife. These days many wives like to join in the sport either as a gun, walking with the beaters or picking up with the family gundog and, in many households, they seem quite happy to do all the plucking. Others choose to stay at home to share the secondhand excitement of the day's sport during the 'action replay' over supper by the fire.

Fit for the Table

Most men can be persuaded to prepare the bag for the table if it is just a brace of birds or a single rabbit or hare, but there are times, such as after a successful day decoying pigeons when the bag is much larger, and in warmer weather when speed is important, when it is a case of many hands making light work. On these occasions every wife should be prepared to muck in. Involving children in the plucking chore can be a time saver once they have practised a few times. Most children are prepared to have a go, especially if a small fee per bird is involved. Bear in mind, though, that their stamina is limited: fingers will tire quickly and many children find the wing and tail feathers too tough, so be prepared to do a little tidying up! However, if the family does not rise to the occasion, you can always pay your local butcher or odd-job man to prepare the game for you. Certainly this is advisable if you have a whole carcass of venison to deal with as few of us have the necessary space, equipment or expertise to prepare so large an animal.

This chapter makes the necessary general points about making game fit for the table; special hints are given for each particular species in the appropriate chapter.

HANGING

The reason for hanging game is to enable the fibres of the flesh to break down so that the meat will become more tender and also to improve the flavour. There is no fast rule which states how long to hang birds or ground game as much depends on the weather and individual tastes of the consumer. A September grouse may need hanging for only two days, whereas a cock pheasant shot in cold January will hang for two to three weeks and still be in perfect condition. Some like to cook or freeze their game within twenty-four hours, while die-hard traditionalists prefer to hang theirs until they are 'high' and the flesh around the vent has turned bluish-green. In extreme cases, a bird is hung until it literally drops off the hook in what many would consider a fairly advanced state of putrefaction. Hanging also increases the 'gamey' flavour, so very young birds will lose their delicate taste if hung for too long.

Weather and personal tastes aside, there are some useful guidelines concerning hanging. Game birds in the United Kingdom are traditionally hung by their necks; the French hang a bird by one leg to allow air to circulate under the feathers. Rabbits and hares are hung by their back legs. Always hang birds individually, with a string tied around the neck, never as a brace, so that the air can circulate freely around each one. A stout nail in a wall makes a perfectly adequate hanging point, but better still is a game hanging rack. Each head of game is hung individually in the angles of a metal, diamond-gridded frame screwed to the wall at an angle. No strings are needed and each bird has a layer of air all round; the bird's own weight holds it firmly in position and the device will take anything from a snipe to a hare. Keep game out of direct sunlight—a cold shed or garage is ideal—and high enough to be out of reach of dogs, cats and rats. During the early part of the season, in blow-fly time, a fly-proof larder is a good investment as without it birds become maggot-ridden within hours of hanging. It is a good idea to keep very badly damaged birds separate from the rest and hang them for a shorter time.

Game birds are traditionally hung by their necks. Rabbits and hares are hung by their back legs

There is much unnecessary mystique surrounding the hanging of game, but there is no doubt that it does improve the flavour and help to tenderise the meat, but the determining time factor must be your individual taste for, after all, you are the consumer!

AGEING

To cook any game successfully it is important to know the age of the bird or animal. Young game is the more desirable as it is tender and suitable for the quicker cooking methods such as roasting, grilling or frying. Older and therefore tougher game needs to be braised, casseroled, pot-roasted or prepared in a pressure cooker.

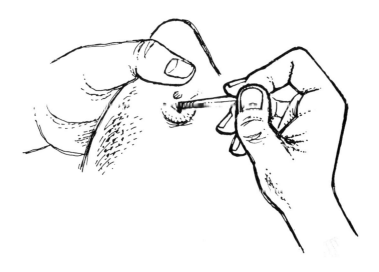

The bursa test, using a blunt matchstick. The bursa can be seen just below the left thumb

There is only one method of ageing which may be applied to all game birds: the bursa test. All young game birds have a small blind-ended passage or bursa, opening just above the vent. To find this, open out the vent area with the thumb, and the bursa, if present, should be clearly seen. The end of a matchstick or quill feather can then be carefully inserted into the bursa. In a young pheasant it will penetrate to a depth of about 2.5cm (1in) and in a young grouse or partridge to a depth of about 1cm (½in). In all species the bursa becomes much reduced or may close completely when the bird is sexually mature.

Each individual game species has additional features which help to distinguish young from old and these will be more fully described in the appropriate chapter.

PLUCKING

Plucking should be done out of doors in a sheltered spot or in a shed or garage as there are bound to be some flying feathers. Wear a large apron or overall and pluck the birds into a large box or dustbin. For larger birds it is a good idea to lay them on a board over the bin.

Start by fanning the wings and pulling out the primaries, then work in towards the body. There is no need to pluck completely the

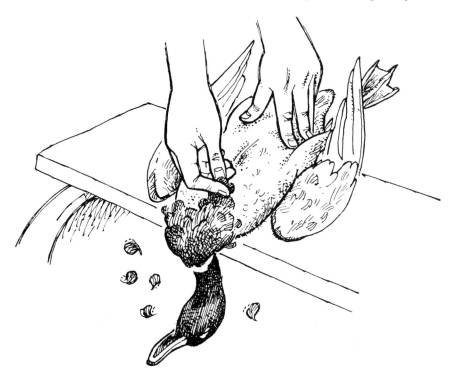

Lay large birds on a board and pluck the feathers into a dustbin

end wing joint of the smaller game birds as there is so little meat on them, so cut off the wing at the joint. The wings of duck may be removed altogether for they carry virtually no flesh and are very tedious to pluck. Likewise, if a wing has been badly damaged it should be cut off completely. Continue with the neck and work down to the tail, pulling the feathers against the grain. Take care not to tear the tender skin on the breast and neck otherwise the meat dries out during cooking. Pull out any remaining quill ends; use pliers for stubborn ones.

SKINNING

If you are using a bird for a pâté, casserole or pie, which will usually be the case if it is badly damaged, or if you require just the breast meat, it is much quicker to skin rather than pluck.

Cut off the head and clip off the wings and legs with secateurs. Lay the bird on its back and, with a sharp knife, cut the skin lightly along the breastbone and peel it off in one piece. This works especially well with wildfowl. Other game birds may shed a few feathers in the process which cling to the flesh, but these can easily

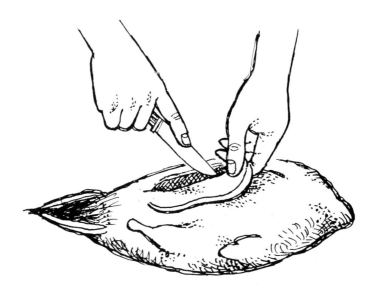

Skinning a duck. Using a sharp knife cut the skin lightly along the breastbone

be washed off under the tap. If you require only the breast meat, simply peel back the skin to expose the breast, then make a cut under the lower end of the breastbone, cut deeply along the ribs close to the wings and then through the collarbones with the secateurs. Remove the whole breast in one piece on the bone.

DRAWING

Before starting this operation, make sure you have all your equipment handy. You will need a small sharp knife, a pair of stout kitchen scissors or an old pair of secateurs, a skewer and a bucket for the intestines. In our household very little is discarded, as what we or the dogs do not eat, the ferrets will!

Using a sharp knife cut off the head at the top of the neck.

Loosen the skin around the neck and draw out the windpipe and crop, being careful to avoid breaking the crop.

Cut off the neck as close to the body as possible, leaving the loose skin intact, to be folded over the back later when trussing.

Make a cut above and below the vent and remove it. Gripping the bird around the breast with the one hand, insert two fingers of the other hand into the body cavity. Reach up under the breastbone and pull out in one clean movement the heart, gizzard, liver, gall-bladder and intestines.

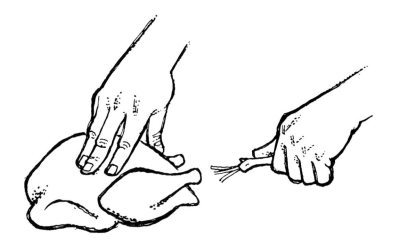

Removing the tendons from the leg of a pheasant

19

Keep the heart, gizzard and liver but discard the intestines and the gall-bladder without puncturing it.

Split the gizzard, peeling off and discarding the lining and contents, and wash in cold water together with the heart, liver and neck and keep them for making stock. The liver may be saved for pâté.

Make a nick across the knee joint, being careful not to cut through the tendons. Break the joint by hand and pull the two ends apart: some of the tendons should draw out, but if they don't, use a skewer to hook them out one at a time.

Wash the bird inside and out under cold running water and dry thoroughly with kitchen paper or a cloth.

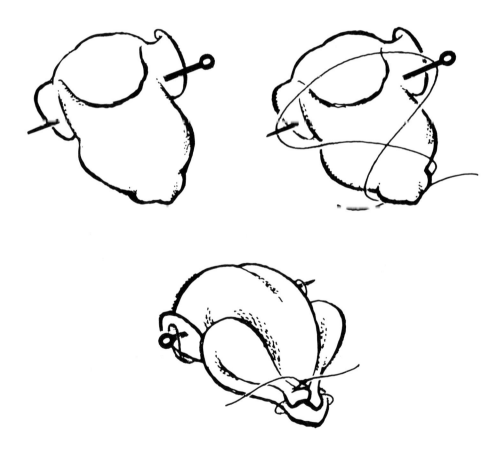

Trussing a pheasant

TRUSSING

The reason for trussing a game bird before roasting is to keep it compact during cooking to help prevent it from drying out. It also improves the appearance of the bird on the table and makes it easier to carve. However, trussing a game bird is often more difficult than a chicken as you will not always have the benefit of a perfect bird; the skin may be torn, a leg or wing broken or missing, so you may have to improvise using skewers and string. For smaller birds, such as grouse and partridge, use cocktail sticks.

Place the bird on its breast and pull back the wings close to the side of the body.

Push a skewer through the wing just below the first joint, through the body and out through the other wing.

Pull back the neck skin.

Take a piece of string about 45cm (18in) long and place around the ends of the skewer, catching the neck flap underneath, then cross the string over the back of the bird and tie it around the parson's nose.

Turn the bird onto its back, pull the legs together and tie the string firmly around the drumsticks, pulling them towards the parson's nose. If the legs are damaged you may have to pass a second skewer through them on which to tie the string.

JOINTING A GAME BIRD

If you wish to cook a bird in portions you will find game shears a very useful investment, but a sharp knife and a sturdy pair of kitchen scissors will do.

Place the bird breast side down on a table or chopping-board. With a small sharp knife cut along the backbone through skin and flesh. With game shears or scissors, cut through the backbone and open the bird. Turn it over, breast up, and continue cutting along the breastbone which will split the bird into two equal halves. You may either leave the backbone in place or remove it altogether, together with any remaining innards. Try also to work out any loose pellets of shot which often lodge under the skin.

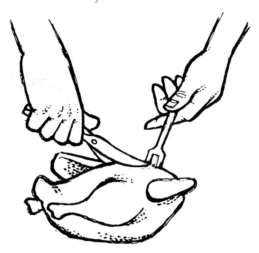

Jointing a gamebird. Cut through the backbone using game shears

FREEZING GAME

Purists prefer to eat only fresh game in season while others are less particular, but one of the virtues of owning a deep freeze is that you can enjoy cooking and eating game at any time of the year. Whatever your feelings, there are times when a freezer is invaluable, for in a shooting household there will be occasions when the bag is too large for your immediate needs. Unless you give away your surplus game, freezing it for future use is the obvious answer.

When preparing a game casserole or soup it is a good idea to cook double the quantity you need and to freeze half of it. 'Eat one and freeze one' will save you time and cooking energy, and you will have a supply of instant meals for those occasions when you are too busy to spend much time in the kitchen. The meal may be defrosted and reheated on the stove or recooked in a microwave oven.

There is no virtue in freezing game in feather and fur unless you are really pushed for time and have a large number to deal with. Feathered game takes up more room in the freezer and, once thawed, plucked and drawn, it must be cooked and not refrozen, although it may be safely frozen after cooking. Pigeon shooters often like to keep a few birds frozen in their feathers to use as decoys.

Birds should be plucked or skinned and drawn. Remove any

visible shot from under the skin, wash them out and dry thoroughly. Wrap in foil or grease-proof paper any sharp protruding bones and pack in heavy-gauge freezer bags or at least two ordinary polythene freezer bags. Alternatively, wrap in aluminium foil, which can be easily moulded to the shape of the bird, then seal in a polythene bag. Expel all the air and seal the bag tightly as any air leaks can cause the meat to dry out.

Finally, label the bag carefully, showing the species, whether young or old and the date. It is also a good idea to include other useful cooking information; for instance, if you have a really clean bird with both legs and wings intact, and the skin untorn, it would be worth indicating that it is suitable for roasting. You may have several young hen pheasants which could be saved for a special occasion, such as a dinner party, in which case label them accordingly. Likewise, an old tough January cock pheasant should be labelled 'casserole' to remind you not to roast it. If you enjoy cooking on a barbecue or open fire in the summer, or wish to grill young game birds or rabbit, these can be jointed and clearly labelled before freezing.

Badly shot birds are best cooked immediately and then frozen for later use in pies or pâté.

Most uncooked game may be stored for between six and nine months, although I have frequently found a 'lost' bird in the bottom of the freezer which had been there for longer than this yet it has still cooked perfectly.

Livers for pâté should be cleaned, have the gall-bladder removed and be packed separately in margarine tubs or polythene bags and may be stored for up to two months uncooked, but only one month if cooked. Cooked game dishes may be frozen for up to three months. It is better to undercook casseroles and add some fresh vegetables when reheating the dish. Roasted birds do not freeze well as the flesh tends to lose moisture and become flabby.

Game pies may be completely cooked before freezing, or the filling only may be cooked and allowed to cool, then topped with pastry and frozen unbaked. They will keep for up to two months. Cooked hot-water crust pastry does not freeze well as it tends to crumble when thawed, and freezing the pastry unbaked can be dangerous as the hot water used to make the pastry might contaminate the meat.

As pâté tends to be highly seasoned it, too, does not freeze well, but if it is sealed with melted butter it will keep for up to two weeks in the refrigerator. Soup freezes well but add starchy ingredients, milk or cream when reheating. Pack in watertight containers, allowing 1cm (½in) head space, and store for two months.

All meat should be allowed to thaw out slowly, preferably overnight, in a cool place.

Finally, try to use game in reverse order of storage, the oldest first, and whenever possible have the freezer empty for the start of each new season.

2

GROUSE

Shooting season: 12 August – 10 December

The red grouse is a rich brown colour speckled with black and white. The hen is duller in colour but more strongly barred than the cock bird. Both have a distinctive red comb, which is more prominent in the cock bird, especially in the breeding season, and feathered legs.

Until recently the red grouse was believed to be the only bird unique to Great Britain, but it is, in fact, closely related to the American willow grouse. It is a native of wild heather moorland and can be found in parts of Scotland, Ireland, Northern Ireland, England and Wales. It has also been successfully introduced to Dartmoor and Exmoor.

Grouse are truly wild birds, but their breeding success depends upon the condition of the moor which provides food, shelter and nesting ground. They feed almost exclusively on berries, and the young shoots, flowers and seed heads of heather. Adult birds tend to favour the current year's growth of young heather plants which are already three years old.

The red grouse tends to be short-lived, as only one in three birds is expected to live longer than a year owing to parasites, predation, shooting and cyclical fluctuations.

Together with snipe, grouse are the first game birds to come into season with the arrival of the glorious twelfth. They are highly sought after, especially on the opening day of the season, when restaurateurs will go to amazing lengths to win the culinary race in which birds are rushed from the moors to distant hotels, so that grouse shot on the moors early that morning may be served for dinner the same evening.

Owing to a diet of heather and berries, grouse has a unique flavour which is enhanced by the plainest cooking, but it also lends itself to more exciting and unusual dishes. The meat is dark and succulent and of a stronger flavour than other game birds.

HANGING

During August and September, when the weather is warm, grouse need hang only for twenty-four hours, although this is not always possible if you live several hundred miles from the moor where they have been shot. Special care must be taken to ensure that the birds hang singly in a cool place where the air can circulate freely; a fly-proof game larder in the shed or garage is ideal. If grouse have spent several hours in the back of the car en route from the moor, it is wise to prepare them for cooking or freezing as soon as possible. Later in the season, when the weather is cooler, they may be hung for five to seven days.

AGEING

For successful cooking, it is most important to be able to distinguish old from young birds, especially if buying from a butcher who himself may not know the difference. Having said this, I can only suggest general guidelines as apart from the fool-proof bursa test described on p16, other methods are less reliable.

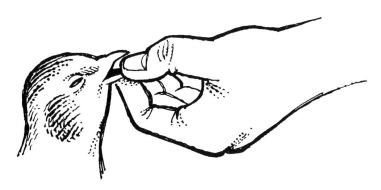

Ageing a grouse. The lower mandible of a young grouse should break if held between the thumb and first finger

Other less reliable methods are to examine the beak, feet and primary or flight feathers. The lower mandible of a young bird should break under the weight of the bird if it is held between the thumb and first finger, although this can only be a certain test at the very beginning of the season.

A more reliable method is to examine the outer primary or flight feathers. Many young birds have the third feather shorter than the rest, and the two outermost feathers on a young bird have pointed lance-shaped tips whereas the others are blunt and rounded. So a bird with all blunt primary feathers is likely to be old.

Another guide is that adult grouse shed their toe-nails some time between July and September, so if a nail is in the process of becoming detached it is a sign of an older bird.

Grouse are in prime condition from the beginning of the season to the middle of October.

When you have determined the age of your grouse, note that only very young birds should be roasted in the traditional English way. Pot-roasting by adding a little water, or the French method with butter and wine, can help to make a bird of uncertain age more tender and moist. As long as they are well basted, young birds are delicious cut in half and grilled or cooked on a barbecue. If in any doubt choose a longer, slower cooking method or use in a pie or pâté.

Grouse can be bought from game dealers and are available from many larger supermarkets from mid-August to late October either fresh or frozen. If you are buying oven-ready, make sure you read the labelling which should indicate the age of the bird.

Grouse

Allow one grouse per person when roasting or grilling. In stews and casseroles, a larger older bird will usually serve two.

Grouse can be stored in a deep freeze for six to eight months.

Roast Grouse   serves 4

There is no doubt that one of the best ways of cooking young grouse in August is to roast them with bacon in a hot oven and serve them with a thin gravy, fruit jelly and young fresh vegetables such as French or runner beans which are cheap and plentiful at this time of year. Grouse have so little natural fat that care must be taken to ensure that the flesh does not become dry. Rashers of streaky bacon placed around the breast and legs will help to keep them moist.

4 young grouse	1 level tbsp cornflour
8 rashers streaky bacon	Black pepper
300ml (½ pint) stock	Watercress for garnish

Tie two bacon rashers around each bird so that the breast and legs are covered.

Place in a roasting tin and cook in a hot oven 200°C (400°F), gas mark 6, for 45 minutes.

Transfer the birds to a serving dish, cover and keep hot.

Blend the cornflour with a little stock and add to the pan. Gradually add the rest of the stock, a shake of pepper and bring to the boil.

Decorate the grouse with watercress and serve with the hot gravy, fried breadcrumbs and cranberry or elderberry jelly (see pp161 and 162).

Grouse may be served on a slice of toast either after cooking, or the toast may be placed under the bird when half cooked to catch the juices.

Pot-roast Grouse   serves 4

Later in the season it is often better to pot-roast older birds for a longer cooking time in a small amount of water, stock or wine. This will help tenderise the meat and keep it moist. Young birds are equally good treated this way. In this particular recipe, apples and bacon are used to add flavour during the cooking. The addition of redcurrant jelly and black pepper is all that is needed to make a delicious gravy.

4 grouse
8 rashers streaky bacon
2 apples, peeled, cored and
  halved

Black pepper
1tbsp redcurrant or crab-apple jelly
Sprigs of parsley or heather to
  garnish

Place half an apple in each bird.

Wrap two rashers of bacon around each bird and place breast side down in a roasting tin. Add water to a depth of 1cm (½in). Cover with foil and roast in a moderate oven, 180°C (350°F), gas mark 4, for 1 hour.

Remove the bacon rashers and turn the birds over. Cover and cook for another 15 minutes.

Roll the bacon rashers and place on an ovenproof serving dish in the top of the oven to brown.

When the grouse are cooked, scoop out the softened apple and place the birds on the serving dish with the bacon rolls. Cover and keep hot.

Pass the apples through a sieve and mix with the pan juices.

Add 1tbsp redcurrant or crab-apple jelly (see p161-2) and black pepper and bring the gravy to the boil.

Serve the grouse decorated with the bacon rolls and sprigs of parsley or heather. Serve the gravy separately.

Grouse Salad   serves 4

The pot-roast method in the previous recipe is similar to the French way of roasting meat and is ideal if you wish to serve grouse cold. Allow the birds to cool completely in the cooking liquid to keep the flesh really moist. There is no need to smother the grouse in a rich salad dressing as this will mask its unique flavour.

Freshly picked English tomatoes, especially the cherry variety, combined with black olives make a colourful salad to accompany the cold grouse.

2 cold grouse
450g (1lb) English tomatoes
50g (2oz) black olives

Salt and freshly milled
  black pepper
Chopped basil to garnish

Remove the meat from the bones and discard the skin. Tear the flesh into shreds and arrange in the centre of a serving dish.

Slice the tomatoes and arrange around the grouse meat. Season with a little salt and black pepper.

Slice the olives in half and remove the stones. Arrange over the tomatoes and sprinkle with chopped basil.

Grilled Grouse   serves 4

Although many people feel it sacrilegious to cook young grouse by any method other than roasting, split in half, they may be grilled successfully or barbecued as long as they are well basted with oil or a marinade during cooking to prevent the meat from becoming dry. In this recipe the birds are marinated for 24 hours in a simple mixture of oil and orange juice.

4 very young grouse	Season-All
3tbsp oil	Orange slices to garnish
3tbsp orange juice	

Combine the oil, orange juice and Season-All in a shallow dish.

Split the grouse in halves, using game shears or kitchen scissors, and trim off any loose bones. Wash thoroughly in cold water, removing any loose pellets under the skin and any remaining innards.

Dry the birds and place them flesh down in the marinade, cover and leave for 24 hours. Occasionally, spoon the marinade over the birds.

Next day, lay the birds flesh side down on the rack in the grill pan and cook under a pre-heated hot grill for about 8 minutes on each side. Baste frequently with the marinade and be careful not to over-cook. The outside skin should be browned, but the flesh still tinged with pink.

Decorate with orange slices, spoon over any remaining juices from the grill pan and serve immediately with plenty of field mushrooms and new potatoes.

Grouse Parcels   serves 4

This is a simple, but delicious way to eat grouse, or any game come to that, provided that it is young, cooked out of doors on a barbecue.

2 young grouse   2tbsp cranberry or
4 rashers bacon   rowanberry jelly

Split the grouse in halves and prepare as in the previous recipe.
   Place each half flesh side up on a square of tin-foil. Add a rasher of bacon and ½tbsp of cranberry or rowan jelly on top. Wrap and seal the foil parcel. Cook for 20-30 minutes.
   Serve with crusty bread and salads.

Grouse in Red Wine   serves 4

This is a classic method of cooking either young or more mature birds and an ideal way to serve grouse when entertaining as it can be prepared in advance, giving you more time to spend with your guests. In this recipe the birds are cut in half before cooking; this is most easily done using a pair of game shears—a good investment if you frequently cook game or poultry.

2-3 grouse, halved   300ml (½pt) red wine
50g (2oz) butter   300ml (½pt) stock
2 small onions, peeled and   225g (8oz) button mushrooms
   chopped   Fresh parsley to garnish
40g (1½oz) flour

Melt the butter in a flameproof casserole and fry the onions and grouse until slightly browned. Remove and set to one side.
   Sir the flour into the melted butter and gradually add the wine and stock, stirring all the time until the sauce thickens.
   Add the grouse, onions, mushrooms and a little salt and pepper if necessary. Cover and simmer slowly for 1-1½ hours, depending on the age of the grouse.
   This can be reheated just before serving, then transferred to a hot serving dish and decorated with fresh parsley.

Ravenseat Grouse serves 4

Another recipe for more mature birds in which a touch of the single malt (no need to mention brand names) adds the spirit of the moors: tumbling burns, lichened rocks and purple heather.

2 old grouse	1 large carrot, sliced
1 chicken stock cube dissolved in 600ml (1pt) water	2tbsp whisky
1 small onion, finely sliced	225g (8oz) chopped mushrooms
	Chopped parsley

Either pressure cook the grouse with the onion, carrot and stock for 30 minutes or simmer in a saucepan for 1 hour.

Remove the birds from the pan and, when cool enough to

Ravenseat Grouse

handle, split them in half and trim away the rib-bones. Place the grouse halves in a casserole.

Liquidise the softened vegetables or pass through a sieve, and add to the casserole together with the remaining stock.

Add the chopped mushrooms, parsley and whisky. Cover and cook in a moderate oven, 180°C (350°F), gas mark 4, for a further 1 hour.

Grouse Pots

Another easy dish to prepare, especially if you have a food processor, and it makes good use of older or damaged birds. Potted grouse makes a smooth filling for sandwiches, and can be spread on toast or savoury biscuits topped with tomatoes to make a tasty snack.

1 old grouse	1tsp lemon juice
4 rashers streaky bacon	1tsp mixed herbs
150ml (¼pt) water	Black pepper
50g (2oz) softened butter or low-fat spread	

Place the grouse in a small saucepan, cover with the bacon rashers and add the water.

Cover and simmer for 1½-2 hours or until tender. Leave the grouse in the saucepan until quite cold.

Remove all the meat from the bones, discarding the skin, chop the bacon and place all the meat in the bowl of a food processor fitted with the metal blade.

Add the softened butter or low-fat spread, lemon juice, mixed herbs and black pepper to taste. Mix until smooth.

If you haven't a processor, pass the cooked meats through a mincer, then mix in the rest of the ingredients and beat until smooth.

Place the mixture in small pots, cover with foil or cling film and store in the refrigerator until required.

Save the remaining stock to use in a sauce or game soup.

Jellied Grouse serves 6

Cooked grouse, ham and hard-boiled eggs, combined with a jellied stock, make an attractive and very easily prepared cold dish which may be served as part of a cold buffet. Use mature birds which have been pot-roasted or pressure cooked, retaining the cooking liquid to make the jellied stock.

2 mature grouse, cooked	1 level tbsp powdered gelatine
225g (8oz) cooked ham	Watercress, sliced tomatoes and
2 hard-boiled eggs	cucumber to garnish
450ml (¾pt) stock	

Dissolve the gelatine in warm stock and leave to cool.

Strip the meat from the carcasses, discarding the skin, and tear into small shreds.

Chop the ham into small pieces and mix with the grouse meat.

Slice the hard-boiled eggs into rings.

Wet a 900ml (1½pt) plastic ring mould and line the base and sides with the egg slices. Add the meat mixture and pour over the jellied stock. Leave to set.

Just before serving, unmould onto a plate, fill the centre with watercress and decorate with slices of tomato and cucumber.

Grouse with Celery and Cider serves 3-4

This is a very good way to cook birds later in the season when they are more likely to be mature. The grouse are braised in cider on a bed of vegetables which are puréed after cooking to make a rich gamey sauce.

1 brace of mature grouse	4 sticks celery, sliced
100g (4oz) bacon, chopped	300ml (½pt) cider
1 small onion, finely chopped	300ml (½pt) stock
1 small parsnip, sliced	Bay leaf

Place the chopped vegetables in a flameproof casserole.

Add the grouse breast side down on the bed of vegetables, bacon and bay leaf. Pour over the stock and cider. Bring slowly to the boil, cover and simmer for 1½-2 hours or until tender.

Grouse

Remove the grouse and bacon from the casserole. Pull off the legs and wings and cut away the breast meat.

Place the grouse meat and bacon on a serving dish, cover with foil and keep hot.

Purée the softened vegetables in a blender or push through a sieve. Return the purée to the casserole and reheat gently.

Pour the sauce over the grouse and serve with glazed carrots and creamed potatoes.

3

PARTRIDGE

Shooting season: 1 September – 1 February

GREY PARTRIDGE

The English, grey or common partridge is a smallish chestnut-brown bird with darker brown and cream bars on flanks and wings. The cock bird has a prominent chestnut horseshoe on its grey breast, but this is less distinctive in the hen bird.

It is found throughout the United Kingdom except on high ground. The grey partridge has suffered a decline owing to changes in farming practices and erosion of its habitat. Its breeding is also affected by bad weather and stocks are maintained by careful protection from predators during the breeding season and restrictions on spraying with insecticides.

Partridge

The red-legged or French partridge is larger than the grey, with olive-brown plumage on its back, distinctive bars on its sides, red bill and legs, and white eye stripe.

It was introduced from France in the seventeenth century, and although it does not breed well in the north of England, in the south it has replaced the grey partridge as the bird of the roots and stubbles.

Its habitat is similar to that of the pheasant and it is more adaptable to changing agricultural methods. It is also more hardy than the grey partridge and also, to some extent, is less affected by bad weather.

The partridge, especially the English or grey bird, is considered by many to be the 'king of game birds', to be chosen in preference to pheasant for its mild and delicate flavour as well as its sporting qualities. This is further endorsed by the old proverb, 'If the partridge had but the woodcocks' thigh, 'twould be the best bird that e'er did fly.'

In her 1888 edition of *The Book of Household Management*, Mrs Isabella Beeton writes, 'Partridge should be chosen young; if old they are valueless. Young birds are generally known by their yellow legs and dark coloured bills.'

This was sound advice to readers, many of whom would buy their game from the local poulterer for about 4s a brace. This was at a time when the English partridge was common, most arable fields holding a covey or two. After a partridge shoot today the bag is likely to contain old as well as young birds and, although Mrs Beeton declares these to be valueless, we can no longer afford to discard them. However, they will require careful cooking as they can be very tough. Use them in a variety of casseroles or in a mixed game pie. Very young birds are exquisite plainly roasted or grilled. Allow one bird per person if possible.

HANGING

Early in the season, especially in a mild autumn, there is no need to hang a partridge for more than three to four days. There may still be blow-flies about, so use a fly-proof larder if you have one. Later in the year when the temperature drops, provided they are hanging so that cool air can circulate freely around them, they may be hung for a week.

English or Grey Partridge

In September and the early part of October, a young bird has a dark beak and creamy yellowish legs, whereas the older bird has a paler grey beak and grey legs. In the later part of the season the flight feather test may be used. In a young bird the two outer primaries have pointed tips, easily distinguished from the more rounded primary feathers of an older bird.

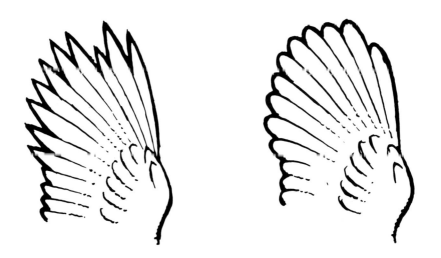

The pointed primary feathers of a young grey partridge (left) may be distinguished from the more rounded primary feathers of an older bird (right)

Red-legged Partridge

The two outer primary feathers on a young bird are tipped with a cream colour. The bursa test described on p16 may be applied to both grey and red-legged partridge. A burnt matchstick should penetrate to a depth of about 1cm (½in) in a young bird.

Partridge are plucked, drawn and trussed before cooking. A

wooden cocktail stick may be used instead of a skewer. Partridge freezes well and may be kept for six to eight months. This prized game bird is available at some large supermarkets from mid-September and is the ideal bird to try if you have never eaten game before.

Roast Partridge   serves 4

In early October the best way to cook young partridge is plainly roasted with a little seasoned butter and streaky bacon to keep them moist.

4 young partridge	Black pepper
8 rashers streaky bacon	Watercress to garnish
50g (2oz) butter	

Season the butter with a little pepper and place a quarter into the body cavity of each bird.

Truss the birds and tie two rashers of streaky bacon across the breast of each bird.

Place in a roasting tin which is just large enough to take the four birds, cover loosely with tin-foil and cook in a fairly hot oven, 200°C (400°F), gas mark 6, for 45 minutes.

Towards the end of the cooking time remove the foil so that the bacon will crisp.

Place the birds on a hot serving dish, pour over the pan juices and garnish with watercress.

Serve with a selection of early winter vegetables such as broccoli or Brussels sprouts.

Grilled Partridge with Mushroom Sauce   serves 4

Provided that they are basted frequently during cooking, very young and therefore tender partridge may be grilled or barbecued. Serve piping hot with a mild-flavoured mushroom sauce which is quickly prepared.

4 very young partridge	100g (4oz) mushrooms, chopped
50g (2oz) melted butter	½tbsp cornflour
1 small can evaporated milk	Salt and black pepper

Partridge

Split the partridge in half using game shears or strong scissors and trim away any small rib-bones. Wash to remove any innards and wipe dry.

Brush all over with melted butter.

Place on the grill rack and cook under a hot pre-heated grill for about 15 minutes, turning and basting frequently. Be careful not to overcook.

Mushroom Sauce

Make the evaporated milk up to 300ml (½pt) with water. Place in a saucepan together with the chopped mushrooms, salt and pepper.

Bring to the boil, then simmer for 10-15 minutes until the mushrooms are soft.

Blend the cornflour in 1tbsp water. Gradually add to the sauce, stirring until thickened.

Pot-roast of Partridge   serves 4

This recipe is equally well suited to both young and mature birds and is a good alternative to a plain roast especially if the birds are of uncertain age. The partridge are cooked in a mixture of stock and orange juice which is used to make the sauce.

4 partridge	1tbsp cornflour
3 large oranges	Salt and pepper
300ml (½pt) stock	Watercress to garnish

Cut one of the oranges into four and place a quarter inside each bird. Truss the birds, securing the legs firmly to the parson's nose, using string.

Place the partridge in a roasting tin or casserole which is just large enough to fit the birds. Add the zest and juice of the second orange together with the stock. Cover with foil or a tight-fitting lid. Cook in a moderate oven, 180°C (350°F), gas mark 4, for 1½-2 hours, depending on the age of the birds.

Remove the partridge from the casserole and split in half, discarding the piece of orange. Place on a serving dish and keep warm.

Blend the cornflour with a little cold water and then add to the gravy with a little salt and pepper. Bring to the boil, stirring all the time, and cook for 2-3 minutes.

Spoon a little of the sauce over the birds and pour the rest into a sauce-boat.

Slice the third orange into rings and use to decorate the dish together with the watercress.

Lord's Ground Partridge   serves 4

Although most people prefer to roast young partridge plainly, this recipe is a little richer and ideal to serve for a special occasion as it may be prepared in advance and frozen if necessary. The flavour of English Cox apples, wine and cream combine well and complement the partridge without overpowering its delicate flavour.

4 young partridge cut in half   150ml (5fl oz) single cream
50g (2oz) butter   Salt and pepper
450g (1lb) Cox apples   Fried apple rings and chopped
300ml (½pt) white wine   parsley to garnish
150ml (¼pt) stock

Cut the partridge in half using game shears or strong kitchen scissors, and trim away the backbone and small rib-bones as much as possible. Wash and dry the birds.

Melt the butter in a flameproof casserole and gently brown the birds. Add the apples, wine, stock and seasoning. Bring to the boil, then simmer gently for about 1 hour.

Remove the birds and keep them hot on a serving dish. Rub the apples through a sieve and return to the casserole.

If you wish to freeze the dish, do so at this stage. Pour the sauce over the partridge joints, allow to cool completely and then prepare for the freezer.

Otherwise, add the cream to the sauce in the casserole and gently heat through. Spoon the sauce over the partridge joints and sprinkle with chopped parsley.

The dish may be decorated with fried apple rings.

Space-age Partridge   serves 4

Game cooking is usually associated with the farmhouse kitchen range, an Aga, or at least a conventional gas or electric cooker, rather than the microwave, which is gradually finding its way into kitchens old and new. Young partridge do not need lengthy cooking as they are usually very tender, so are suitable for use in the microwave. This recipe was prepared using an oven with a 650W output, power control levels 1-9, with an automatic turntable and stirrer fan. Times for 500W and 600W ovens are also included at the end of the recipe.

2 young partridge, split in halves	Zest and juice of 1 lemon
4 rashers streaky bacon, chopped	25g (1oz) cornflour
1 small onion, chopped	Black pepper
225g (8oz) mushrooms	Chopped parsley and lemon
15g (½oz) butter	butterflies to garnish
300ml (½pt) game stock	

Place the bacon, onion and 15g (½oz) butter in a 2.25 litre (4pt) round ovenproof or glass ceramic casserole. Cover and cook on PL9 for 4 minutes (a).

Add the partridge halves, with the thinner leg ends towards the centre, the zest of the lemon and pepper, and pour over the stock. Cover and cook on PL9 for 10 minutes (b).

Add the chopped mushrooms. Cover and cook on PL4 for 25 minutes (c).

Blend the cornflour with the lemon juice, add to the casserole and cook covered on PL9 for 10 minutes (d).

Serve straight from the casserole garnished with chopped parsley and lemon butterflies.

Microwave times

500W	600W	650W
a) 7min	a) 6min	a) PL9 4min
b) 20min	b) 16min	b) PL9 10min
c) 20min on full power	c) 25min on defrost	c) PL4 25min
d) 10min	d) 10min	d) PL9 10 min

Partridge and Pears   serves 4

English Conference pears are plentiful during October and November and their flavour combines well with partridge. They are poached together in stock and red wine to make a colourful dish.

4 young partridge	25g (1oz) butter
150ml (¼pt) stock	1 tbsp flour
150ml (¼pt) red wine	4tbsp natural yoghurt
4 firm Conference pears,	Salt and pepper
peeled and halved	Watercress to garnish

Melt the butter in a large flameproof casserole and brown the partridge.

Add the stock, wine, salt and pepper and bring to the boil.

Add the pears and simmer gently for 1 hour or until the birds are tender.

Remove the partridge and pears from the casserole and arrange on a serving dish. Cover and keep hot.

Thicken the sauce with the flour, blended with a little cold water. Adjust the seasoning if necessary.

Add the yoghurt and heat gently, but do not allow the sauce to boil.

Partridge and Pears

43

Pour a little of the sauce over each partridge and decorate with the watercress.

Serve with creamed potatoes and spiced red cabbage (see p170-1). Hand the rest of the sauce separately.

Partridge Salad   serves 4

When preparing game birds for a cold dish it is a good idea to cook them in water or stock and allow them to cool in the cooking liquid. This helps to keep the flesh moist.

4 partridge	1 bayleaf
1 small onion, chopped	Salt and pepper
1 stick celery, chopped	

Place the birds breast side down in a large saucepan. Add the chopped onion, celery, bay leaf and seasoning. Cover the pan, bring to the boil, and simmer for about 1 hour or until tender.

Turn off the heat and leave to cool in the liquid. Remove the partridge when quite cold, drain and serve with red and white slaw or crunchy nut salad (see p169-70).

Retain the stock and use for a soup or casserole.

Partridge Pie   serves 4

Mature partridge may be very tough and need plenty of cooking to ensure tenderness. In this recipe the birds are pre-cooked in either a pressure cooker or simmered on a low heat. Any assortment of winter vegetables may be added together with bacon to give extra flavour.

Brace mature partridge	450ml (¾pt) stock
100g (4oz) bacon, derinded and chopped	1 bay leaf
	1 sprig thyme
1 small onion, finely chopped	225g (8oz) shortcrust pastry
2 carrots, diced	Beaten egg

Place the partridge, chopped bacon, stock, onion, carrots, bay leaf and thyme in a saucepan or flameproof casserole. Bring to the boil, then simmer on a very low heat for 1½ hours or until the birds are tender.

When cool, pull off the legs and cut away the breast and wing sections from the carcasses.

Place a funnel in the centre of a 1.2 litre (2pt) pie dish. Arrange the partridge joints and bacon in the dish, then add the vegetables and stock. Cover with the pastry, brush with beaten egg and cook in a hot oven, 220°C (425°F), gas mark 7, for 45 minutes or until golden brown.

4

PHEASANT

Shooting season: 1 October – 1 February

In Britain, the pheasant is probably the best known and most easily recognised of all game birds either in the field, on the grass verges of a country road, or hanging resplendent on a market stall or butcher's shop window.

The pheasant is a large conspicuous game bird, the cock having flamboyant colourings of glossy green and shiny chestnut. With its red wattles, white neck ring and long tail, it is easily identified and surely universally known. The hen is smaller and less colourful with mottled plumage ranging from light buffs to dark browns.

The pheasant was introduced to this country during the Roman occupation and is now common throughout the United Kingdom except on very high ground. It favours low wooded farmland, forest edges and fen country, and it will travel widely in search of food. Reared birds are often artificially fed, and holding crops are grown for food as well as cover.

HANGING

It is difficult to state firmly exactly how long to hang a pheasant. A young bird shot in October will only need three days, whereas in January, two weeks would not be too long. Make sure that birds are hung singly from their necks, in a cool place where the air can circulate freely.

AGEING

The only certain method of ageing a cock or hen pheasant is the bursa test (see p16). A tapered matchstick or quill should penetrate the bursa about 2.5cm (1in). A cock bird in its first year may be distinguished by its short rounded spurs; these will be more pointed in its second year, and after that they will be long and sharp. A young hen has soft feet which become hard and rough with age.

Short, rounded spurs of a cock bird in its first year (left); pointed spur of a cock bird in its second year (right)

Pheasants are presented by the brace, one cock and one hen, although supermarkets often select hen pheasants only for their oven-ready range. For cooking, many people prefer the hen to the cock as it is considered to be more tender and better flavoured. However, young cock birds can be excellent when roasted and lend

47

themselves to many casserole recipes. Whereas a hen pheasant will only serve two, a good-sized cock will serve three when roasted and can be stretched to serve four in a casserole with plenty of added vegetables. Pheasants are usually in prime condition in late autumn after feeding well on a varied diet of vegetable and animal food. They are available from game dealers and supermarkets from mid-October until the end of January.

Special care must be taken when plucking as the skin tears easily. Truss a pheasant as described on p21. Remember to keep a few tail feathers which may be stuck in a small potato and placed in the body cavity to make an impressive decoration for roast birds.

Although only young birds should be roasted, this does not mean you may not use them for other recipes. Any chicken recipe may be adapted for pheasant. The meat is darker than chicken with a distinctive gamey flavour, dark on the legs and wings and whiter on the breast. Roast the birds breast down so that the juices run into the breast and not off it.

An invaluable item of equipment for pot-roasting and stews is an oval casserole just large enough to hold one cock pheasant, with a snug-fitting lid. The enamelled cast iron type is ideal as it may also be used on top of the oven.

Pheasant is probably the most versatile of all the game birds as it combines so well with a variety of vegetables, fruits, herbs and spices, and is excellent in game pies, pâtés and soups. Pheasant may be stored in the freezer for about nine months.

Roast Pheasant   serves 4

There are various ways of roasting pheasants, either wrapped in bacon or foil, in a chicken brick, on a trivet or French roasted with wine and butter. All these methods can be delicious, and there is no doubt that simple roasting is one of the best ways of cooking a pheasant. In this recipe a self-basting roasting tin is used, and the birds are cooked breast down so that the juices run into and not off the succulent breast meat. The birds are uncovered and turned for the final stage of cooking to brown the skin.

Pheasant

2 young pheasants

Traditional Accompaniments
Game chips   Fresh cranberries, parsley and
Fried breadcrumbs   pheasant tail feathers for decoration

Truss the pheasants and place breast down in a self-basting roasting tin. Cover and cook in a moderately hot oven, 200°C (400°F), gas mark 6, for 1 hour.

Remove the lid, turn the pheasants and return to the oven for a further 15 minutes to allow the birds to brown. Transfer to a hot serving dish.

Make a thin gravy using the juices from the pan and serve this separately, together with the traditional accompaniments of game chips and fried breadcrumbs (see p161). Decorate the birds with fresh cranberries, parsley and pheasant tail feathers.

Microwave Roast Pheasant   serves 2

It is possible to roast a pheasant or any young game bird in a microwave oven either using a roaster bag or placed directly in a dish and loosely covered with greaseproof paper. With the second method, microwave the pheasant breast side down for the first half of the cooking time.

1 young pheasant   Ground paprika
25g (1oz) soft margarine or butter 10ml (2 level tsp) flour

Truss the pheasant using string and a wooden skewer. Spread the margarine or butter over the pheasant and sprinkle lightly with paprika.

Sprinkle the flour inside the roaster bag and place the pheasant inside. Tie the bag loosely with string, making sure there is room for the steam to escape.

Weigh the pheasant, then stand on a dish. Microwave on medium (60 per cent of full power) for 9 minutes to the 450g (1lb).

Leave to stand for 15 minutes before unwrapping. Use the cooking juices to make a thin gravy and serve with traditional accompaniments.

Roast Pheasant with Celery and Nut Stuffing serves 4-6

It is not usual to stuff game birds in the same way as turkey or chicken, though a piece of onion, apple, orange or lemon may be placed inside the body cavity. The birds may be boned out and then filled with a stuffing, reshaped and trussed. Here the stuffing is cooked around the pheasants.

2 young pheasants	6 rashers streaky bacon

For the Stuffing

50g (2oz) fresh breadcrumbs	1 egg, beaten
1 stick celery, finely chopped	2tbsp lemon juice
1 onion, finely chopped	Freshly ground black pepper
50g (2oz) chopped salted peanuts	

Mix together breadcrumbs, celery, onion, peanuts and pepper in a basin. Bind the ingredients together with the beaten egg and lemon juice. Form the stuffing into balls.

Truss the pheasants and place breast down in a roasting tin. Lay three rashers of bacon across the back of each bird and place the stuffing balls around the birds. Cover and cook in a moderately hot oven 200°C (400°F), gas mark 6, for 1 hour.

Turn the birds, roll the bacon rashers and return to the oven uncovered and cook for a further 15 minutes so that the bacon rolls and pheasants may brown.

Place the pheasants on a serving dish and decorate with the bacon rolls and stuffing.

Pheasant Supreme serves 4

Pheasant breasts and mushrooms are poached in stock. The addition of brandy and cream makes this a more extravagant dish suitable for a special occasion. One pheasant breast is sufficient for a modest appetite, but a good eater will probably manage two. This recipe is for six breasts which should serve four people generously.

6 pheasant breasts, skinned	1½tbsp cornflour
225g (8oz) mushrooms	Salt and pepper
300ml (½pt) pheasant stock	Watercress or parsley for
300ml (½pt) single cream	decoration
2tbsp brandy	

Using a sharp knife, cut the breasts from the pheasants and remove the skin. Keep the legs and wings for use in a casserole or pie and use the carcasses to make a good stock.

Measure 300ml (½pt) of the stock into a saucepan and add the pheasant breasts, mushrooms, salt and pepper. Bring to the boil and simmer gently for 30 minutes or until the meat is tender.

Remove the pheasant and mushrooms, arrange on a serving dish, cover and keep hot.

Blend the cornflour with a little of the cream, add some warm stock from the saucepan and gradually return to the pan with the rest of the cream. Add the brandy and, stirring continuously, simmer gently for 5 minutes.

Pour the sauce over the pheasant, decorate with watercress or parsley and serve immediately.

Pot-roast Pheasant   serves 4

During January it is usually the custom to shoot only cock pheasants. These may well be mature birds which need long, slow cooking. Pot-roasting is an easy economical way to prepare a hearty meal for the family on a cold winter's day, especially if you are a working mother. Just add the jacket potatoes, set the oven timer and come home to a ready-cooked meal.

1 mature cock pheasant	600ml (1pt) stock
2 large carrots, chopped	2tsp mixed herbs
2 leeks, sliced	Salt and pepper
2 large parsnips, sliced	4 large potatoes, scrubbed
1 green pepper, deseeded and chopped	

Place the pheasant in a large oval casserole, add the chopped vegetables, herbs, seasoning and stock. Cover and place in the centre of the oven.

Scrub four large potatoes, prick with a fork and place at the top of the oven. Cook in a moderate oven, 180°C (350°F), gas mark 4, for 2 hours.

Place the pheasant on a serving dish surrounded by the vegetables, and pour the gravy into a sauce-boat. Serve the jacket potatoes with soured cream or grated cheese.

Pheasant in Red Wine   serves 4

Tender young hen pheasants cooked in red wine with mushrooms served with spiced red cabbage and château potatoes make an ideal menu for entertaining as they can all be cooked in advance and re-heated just before your guests arrive.

2 young hen pheasants	Rind and juice of 1 orange
450ml (¾pt) red wine	1 tbsp cornflour
100g (4oz) mushrooms	Salt and pepper
1 onion, finely chopped	Parsley to garnish

Using game shears or strong kitchen scissors, cut the birds in half and carefully remove the backbone.

Place the birds in a flameproof casserole, add the onion, mushrooms and 300ml (½pt) of the wine. Cook in a moderate oven, 180°C (350°F), gas mark 4, for 1 hour.

Remove the birds from the casserole and place on a serving dish. Arrange the mushrooms around the pheasants, cover with foil and keep hot.

To prepare the sauce, add thinly pared strips of orange rind to the liquid in the casserole, bring to the boil and simmer for 5 minutes. Remove the rind.

Blend the cornflour with a little of the remaining wine, then add to the sauce, together with the rest of the wine, juice of the orange, salt and pepper. Slowly bring to the boil, stirring all the time.

Pour the sauce over the pheasants and decorate with parsley.

Serve with spiced red cabbage and château potatoes (see pp170 and 171).

Pheasant Normande   serves 4

The flavour of pheasant combines perfectly with apples and the addition of a little yoghurt makes a good sauce. This recipe is equally well suited to both young and more mature birds; 30 minutes in a pressure cooker is an ideal way to tenderise an older bird before proceeding with the recipe.

1 large pheasant	2 tbsp natural yoghurt
2 large Cox apples, peeled, cored and sliced	Salt and pepper
	Chopped parsley to garnish
300ml (½pt) dry cider	

Place the pheasant breast down in a flameproof casserole. Add the cider, apples and seasoning and bring to the boil. Cover and simmer for 1-2 hours, depending on the age of the pheasant.

Remove the pheasant and carve onto a serving dish. Cover and keep warm.

Rub the apples through a sieve and return to the casserole.

Bring the sauce to the boil, turn off the heat and stir in the yoghurt.

Pour the sauce over the pheasant and sprinkle with chopped parsley.

Fenland Pheasant   serves 4

As the majority of the pheasants that I cook come from the Fens, and as apples, celery and onions grow in abundance there, the name of this recipe seems appropriate. It is also suitable for a dinner party as it can be made in advance and frozen if necessary. If you or your guests are weight-watchers, use natural yoghurt instead of cream.

1 brace pheasants	1 glass white wine
2 dessert apples, peeled, cored and sliced	150ml (¼pt) single cream or natural yoghurt
3 sticks celery, chopped	1 tbsp cornflour
1 onion, finely sliced	Salt and pepper
450ml (¾pt) stock	Celery leaves for decoration

Place the pheasants breast down in a flameproof casserole. Add the sliced apples, celery and onion, then pour over the stock and wine. Simmer on top of the cooker for about 1½ hours or until the birds are tender.

Remove the pheasants from the casserole and keep them warm. Liquidise the sauce or push the apples and vegetables through a sieve.

Blend the cornflour into the sauce, return to the casserole and slowly bring to the boil, stirring until the sauce thickens. Add the cream or yoghurt and seasoning to taste, and heat through very gently.

Carve the birds onto a serving dish and spoon the sauce over the meat. Decorate with the celery leaves.

Spiced Pheasant with Walnuts   serves 6-8

Apples and fennel are combined with crunchy walnuts to give a pleasant texture to the sauce which is served with the spiced pheasants.

Brace of pheasants	450g (1lb) cooking apples
2tsp soft dark-brown sugar	1 x 225g (8oz) bulb fennel
1tsp ground black pepper	100g (4oz) walnut pieces
3tsp ground mixed spice	150ml (¼pt) orange juice
1tbsp oil	

Mix the sugar, pepper and mixed spice with the oil to make a paste, and spread over the pheasants. Cover and leave overnight in a cool place.

Peel, core and slice the apples. Slice the fennel into thin rings.

Place the walnuts, apples, fennel and orange juice in the bottom of a roasting tin (the self-basting kind is ideal). Place the pheasants on top. Cover with a lid or foil and cook in a moderately hot oven, 190°C (375°F), gas mark 5, for 1¾ hours. Remove the cover for the final 15 minutes of cooking time.

Place the pheasants on a carving dish. Strain the gravy into a gravy-boat and serve the apple, fennel and walnut mixture as a separate sauce.

Spiced Pheasants with Walnuts

Cold Pheasant in Lemon Sauce   serves 4

When preparing a cold pheasant dish, instead of roasting the bird
and leaving it to cool, cook it in water with an onion, bay leaf and
seasoning and allow it to cool in the liquid after cooking. This will
keep the flesh moist. The stock is used to prepare the delicately
flavoured sauce. This is a good recipe for a cold buffet party as it can
easily be made the day before and stored in the refrigerator overnight.

1 pheasant	Few sprigs of parsley
1 small chopped onion	Salt and pepper
Bay leaf	

For the Sauce

300ml (½pt) pheasant stock	1 tbsp cornflour
Zest and juice of 1 lemon	Salt and pepper
300ml (½pt) natural yoghurt or	Sliced cucumber and paprika
single cream	for decoration
1 egg yolk	

Place the pheasant in a saucepan, add the chopped onion, parsley,
bay leaf, salt and pepper, and enough water to just cover the bird.
Bring to the boil and then simmer gently for 1½ hours or until tender. Turn off the heat and leave the pheasant to cool in the liquid.

When cold, remove the meat from the carcass, tear into small
pieces and arrange on a serving plate.

Measure 300ml (½pt) of the pheasant stock and pour most of it
into a saucepan. Add the cornflour to the remainder and blend into
the stock. Bring to the boil, stirring continuously. Simmer for
5 minutes.

Stir in the zest and juice of the lemon, egg yolk and seasoning,
and heat gently for 1 minute.

Remove from the heat and stir in the yoghurt or cream. Allow the
sauce to cool and thicken and then spoon over the pheasant.

Cover and leave in a cool place for 2 hours, or store overnight in
the refrigerator.

Before serving, decorate the dish with slices of cucumber and
dust the pheasant and sauce with paprika.

Cold Pheasant with Apricot and Yoghurt Dressing   serves 4

The addition of apricots gives a tangy flavour to this low-calorie dressing for cold pheasant.

1 pheasant	Sprigs of parsley
1 small onion, chopped	Salt and pepper
Bay leaf	

For the Dressing

300ml (½pt) natural yoghurt	Wedges of tomato, a few lettuce
2 tbsp low-calorie salad dressing	leaves and chopped parsley for
6 whole canned apricots	decoration

Prepare the pheasant as in the previous recipe. You will not need the stock, so keep this for a soup or casserole.

Remove the meat from the carcass, break into small pieces and place in a bowl.

Place the ingredients for the dressing in a liquidiser and blend for 30 seconds. If you haven't a liquidiser, rub the apricots through a sieve and mix the purée with the yoghurt and salad dressing.

Pour the dressing over the pheasant meat and mix thoroughly with a spoon.

Arrange the pheasant meat on a bed of lettuce on a serving dish, sprinkle with chopped parsley and decorate with wedges of tomato.

Easy Pheasant Pâté   serves 6

Any odd pheasant portions or just whole legs may be used for this pâté. Use as a starter, for a picnic or snack.

225g (8oz) pheasant meat—	50g (2oz) streaky bacon, chopped
a whole breast or 6 legs	1 clove garlic, crushed
150ml (¼pt) red wine	Pinch of grated nutmeg
Salt and pepper	Black pepper
225g (8oz) minced pork	

Cook the pheasant in the wine and seasoning for about 30 minutes. Allow to cool, then remove the meat from the bones. Tear into small pieces and place in a mixing bowl. Reserve the cooking liquid.

Add the minced pork, chopped streaky bacon, garlic, nutmeg and black pepper to the pheasant meat. Mix together with enough of the cooking liquid to give a moist consistency.

Place in a wetted terrine or loaf tin and cover with a lid or tin-foil. Stand in a baking tin half filled with hot water and bake for 1¼ hours in a moderate oven, 180°C (350°F), gas mark 4.

Allow to cool overnight and serve sliced with toast, crackers or bread.

Devilled Pheasant   serves 4

This is a good way to cook damaged birds with perhaps a missing leg or wing rather than a sound one which would be more suited to roasting. Alternatively, use up any whole legs left over from a 'breast only' recipe. The cooked pheasant is served in a spicy sauce with boiled rice.

1 pheasant or 6 pheasant legs	Bay leaf
1 small onion, chopped	Salt and pepper
1 clove garlic, crushed	

For the sauce

3 tbsp chutney: apple, plum or mango	2tbsp soy sauce
	150ml (¼pt) pheasant stock
1 tbsp Worcestershire sauce	150ml (¼pt) natural yoghurt
1tbsp tomato ketchup	Tomato wedges for decoration

Place the pheasant breast down in a saucepan or small flameproof casserole, add the onion, garlic, bay leaf and seasoning and about 600ml (1pt) water. Bring to the boil and simmer for about 1½ hours or until tender.

When cool enough to handle, remove all the meat from the bones and place in a shallow ovenproof serving dish.

Strain the stock and measure out 150ml (¼pt) for the sauce.

Mix together all the other ingredients for the sauce and gradually blend in the stock.

Pour the sauce over the pheasant meat, cover the dish with a lid or foil and reheat in a moderate oven, 180°C (350°F), gas mark 4, for 30 minutes.

Decorate with wedges of tomato and serve with boiled rice.

Pheasant and Chestnut Pie   serves 4

This is a good way to use up pheasant legs left over from a recipe requiring breasts only. The addition of chestnuts, tomatoes and a
shortcrust pastry makes a nourishing meal for a winter's evening.

6 pheasant legs	2tbsp crab-apple or redcurrant
350g (12oz) fresh chestnuts,	jelly
peeled	Salt and pepper
400g (14oz) tin tomatoes	225g (8oz) shortcrust pastry
1 clove garlic	Beaten egg

In a saucepan, crush a clove of garlic with a little salt. Add the
pheasant legs, tomatoes and juice, peeled chestnuts, redcurrant or
crab-apple jelly (see p161) and a good shake of pepper. Cover the
saucepan and bring to the boil, then simmer for 1 hour or until the
pheasant is tender. Allow to cool.

Place a funnel in the centre of a 1.2 litre (2pt) pie dish.

Strip all the meat from the pheasant legs, taking care to discard
the tough sinews from the lower part of the leg.

Place the meat in the pie dish and add the chestnuts, tomatoes
and gravy. This should just fill the dish. Cover with the shortcrust
pastry. Make a small hole in the centre and decorate with the pastry
trimmings. Brush the pastry with the beaten egg and bake in a hot
oven, 220°C (425°F), gas mark 7, for 45 minutes or until golden
brown.

Serve with creamed potatoes and a green vegetable.

Pheasant Liver Pâté   serves 6

If you find the flavour of pheasant livers too strong, try mixing
them half and half with chicken livers; these are often available
from larger supermarkets. If you seal the pâté with melted butter, it
will keep for up to a fortnight in the refrigerator.

100g (4oz) pheasant livers	1tsp mixed herbs
100g (4oz) chicken livers	1tbsp sherry
1 small onion, finely chopped	1tbsp milk
1 clove garlic, crushed	Freshly ground black pepper
50g (2oz) butter or soft margarine	Fresh bay leaves for decoration
¾tsp grated nutmeg	

Sauté the onion and garlic in 25g (1oz) of the butter. Add the livers, cover and cook over a low heat for 10 minutes.

Cool slightly and purée, using a sieve or blender. Melt the rest of the butter, add the seasonings, sherry and milk. When heated through, add to the liver purée and blend until the consistency of whipped cream.

Spoon the pâté into an earthenware dish. Cover and chill for at least 2 hours.

Decorate with fresh bay leaves and serve with toast and salad.

Pheasant Burgers   serves 4

Burgers are easy to make from the tougher leg meat of a roast pheasant or left-overs from a casserole. They make a change from the more usual ham- or beefburgers. For a tasty snack, serve them in baps with ketchup and salad or with chips and baked beans for a popular children's meal.

100g (4oz) cooked pheasant meat (about 2 whole legs)	1tsp mixed herbs
	Salt and pepper
225g (8oz) sausagemeat	1 egg, beaten
1 small onion	Dry breadcrumbs

Mince the pheasant meat and onion or chop in a food processor.

Add the sausagemeat, herbs, salt and pepper and mix thoroughly. Bind together with the beaten egg.

Divide the mixture into four and shape into flat cakes. Coat thoroughly with breadcrumbs.

Fry in oil for 5 minutes on each side or until golden brown.

5

SNIPE AND WOODCOCK

SNIPE
Shooting season: 12 August – 31 January

Only the common snipe is legal quarry, the smaller jack snipe now being a protected species. Both sexes have a light cream breast flecked with brown. The back is dark brown and black with cream stripes. The snipe, a small wader, has a very long bill used to find the insects, worms and water snails it loves.

The snipe is common throughout the United Kingdom inhabiting marshes, boggy moors and damp pastures. It presents a difficult shot as it flies off on a zigzagging course and a shooter who brings one home feels justifiably pleased with himself.

Snipe are one of the smallest of the game birds and considered very much a delicacy. Despite their small size they have large appetites and spend most of the day feeding. They prosper on a diet of worms and water snails, so by October or November they make a well-flavoured bird for the table.

Snipe and Woodcock

WOODCOCK
Shooting season:
England and Wales, 1 October – 31 January
Scotland, 1 September – 31 January

The woodcock is a medium-sized wader with a long straight bill, a large eye and plumage of every conceivable shade of brown which provides an excellent camouflage against the dead leaves of a winter woodland.

Woodcock favour moist woodland with low cover and may be found throughout much of Britain, although they are more common in East Anglia where they arrive after their autumn migration from Scandinavia and the Baltic. After regaining their strength, they then move westwards to Cornwall and eventually over the Irish Sea.

Over the centuries the woodcock has been given a variety of names: the Anglo-Saxons called it *wudecoc*; Linnaeus named it *Scolopax rusticola*, 'the stake-pointed country dweller', and the Dorset man knew it as ditch-owl. To us all, however, it is the woodcock, a strange creature of dawn and dusk, shrouded in mystery, in the bag a cause for pride, on the table a dish fit for a king. It is an elusive bird, wild and untameable, the true ephemeral, here today and who knows where tomorrow.

Woodcock can be testing targets for the shooting man and a 'right and left' is a celebrated feat, the equivalent of a golfer's hole-in-one or an athlete's four-minute mile. It is considered such a rarity that until 1983, any shooter who could provide two witnesses to this feat could claim membership of the 'Bols Snippen Club', a free badge and a bottle of liqueur. This has now been superseded by the Shooting Times Woodcock Club.

Snipe are in season from 12 August, but they are not at their best until October or November, by which time woodcock may also be shot. The condition of both birds may deteriorate during prolonged cold weather as they may be short of food and their fat reserves will be used up. As with all game, hanging is a purely personal matter; this may be for two to four days, depending on the weather, although some people prefer not to hang snipe or woodcock at all. Both birds must be plucked very carefully as the skin is tender and tends to tear easily. Traditionally, snipe and woodcock are not drawn before cooking.

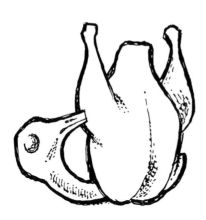

Trussing a woodcock using the beak as a skewer

Skin the head and remove the eyes with a sharp knife. Leave the intestines or 'trail' intact as this liquefies when heated and mingles with the cooking juices. Make a small cut in the side of the bird above the thigh but below the breastbone and with one finger locate and hook out the gizzard. Press the legs and wings together and twist the head around to the side so that the beak may be passed through the legs and body like a skewer.

Pass a piece of string under the body, around the beak which acts as a skewer, cross over the ends and tie round the legs.

Tie a rasher of streaky bacon over the breast. Fry or toast a slice of bread on one side only and stand the bird on the untoasted side so that it will retain the delicate juices released during cooking. Alternatively, place it on a croûton of bread after cooking. Serve with a clear gravy made from the juices and a glass of white wine or a few drops of brandy or lemon juice.

If the 'trail' is too much for you, remove the head and serve in the same way as other game birds. As both birds are too small to be shared, they may be prepared and cooked exactly to individual taste, but they are probably best medium to well done.

Snipe and woodcock are rarely available over the counter or from game dealers as they are usually too highly prized by the shooter and scarce.

Both birds may be frozen, drawn or undrawn, and stored for six to eight months.

Roast Snipe serves 2

These delicately flavoured birds may be left undrawn except for the gizzard, the head skinned and the long beak used as a skewer, or they may be drawn if preferred.

A couple of snipe   Oil and butter for frying
2 streaky bacon rashers   Lemon wedges to garnish
2 slices bread

Wrap a streaky bacon rasher around each bird and place in a small casserole. Cover and cook in a hot oven, 220°C (425°F), gas mark 7, for 15 minutes.

Remove the lid from the casserole, take off the bacon and baste the snipe with the juices. Return to the oven for a further 10 minutes.

Fry the bread in oil and butter until crisp and golden on both sides. When cooked, place each bird on a croûton on a hot serving dish and baste with the pan juices.

Serve immediately, garnished with lemon wedges.

Snipe on Toast serves 2

Though tiny birds, a couple of snipe (never called a brace) will provide a meal of quality if not quantity. It has been said that Winston Churchill's favourite breakfast was a couple of snipe on toast washed down with champagne.

A couple of snipe   Melted butter
2 rashers bacon   Pepper
2 slices bread   2 sprigs of parsley to garnish

Toast the bread on one side only. Place the snipe on the untoasted side of the bread and put them in the bottom of the grill pan. Place a rasher of bacon over the breast of each bird. Cook under a hot grill for 10 minutes or until the bacon is crisp.

Remove the bacon, baste with melted butter and add a shake of pepper. Reduce the heat and continue to cook for 5 minutes.

Place each snipe on toast onto a hot plate, spoon some of the pan juices over each bird and serve with the bacon and a sprig of parsley.

Woodcock Appetiser   serves 4

Cold woodcock, served with a cool cucumber and curd cheese dressing, makes an impressive savoury starter to a meal. After cooking, leave the birds to cool in the stock to prevent the meat from becoming dry.

A couple of woodcock, drawn	*Dressing*
300ml (½pt) stock	100g (4oz) diced cucumber
Sprig of thyme	100g (4oz) curd cheese
Bay leaf	3tbsp natural yoghurt
Salt and pepper	
Lettuce leaves, tomato wedges	
and white grapes to garnish	

Place the woodcock in a small saucepan and add the stock, herbs and seasoning. Cover with a lid, bring to the boil and simmer gently for 40-45 minutes. Leave the birds to cool in the stock, preferably overnight.

Split the birds in half with a sharp knife, trim away the backbone and small rib-bones and remove any remaining innards.

Blend the yoghurt and curd cheese and add the diced cucumber.

To serve, lay each woodcock half on a bed of lettuce on an individual plate. Decorate with tomato wedges and grape halves. Serve the dressing separately.

Woodcock Appetiser

Roast Woodcock serves 2

As a couple of woodcock in the bag is likely to be a rare occurrence, treat the birds with the deference they deserve. They are best served plainly roasted, but a little white wine or brandy may be added to the cooking juices.

A couple of woodcock
2 rashers streaky bacon
2 slices bread
Butter and oil for frying

1 small glass white wine or a
  very little brandy
Lemon wedges to garnish

Prepare the birds in the traditional way (see p61-2) or, if preferred, draw and truss them as for any small game bird.

Place the birds in a small roasting tin or casserole. Cover with foil or a lid and cook in a hot oven, 220°C (425°F), gas mark 7, for 45 minutes.

Uncover the birds, remove the bacon and baste thoroughly with the cooking juices. Cook for a further 15 minutes.

Meanwhile, fry the bread in the oil and butter until crisp and golden brown.

Place the woodcock on the croûtons and keep hot on a serving dish.

Add a little wine or brandy to the cooking juices and then pour this over the birds. Serve immediately garnished with lemon wedges.

Woodcock with Orange Sauce serves 2

A good way to prepare woodcock if you prefer to draw your birds. Pot-roasting in white wine and orange juice keeps the flesh moist.

A couple of woodcock
1 glass dry white wine
Zest and juice of 1 large orange
2tbsp single cream

2tsp cornflour
Salt and pepper
Watercress and orange slices to
  garnish

Truss the birds with string and place them in a small roasting tin or flameproof casserole. Add the wine and zest and juice of the orange. Cover with foil or a lid and cook in a fairly hot oven, 200°C (400°F), gas mark 6, for 1 hour.

Uncover the birds for the final 15 minutes of the cooking time to allow them to brown. Remove the woodcock from the tin and keep hot on a serving dish.

Blend the cornflour with the cream, then stir into the pan juices and heat gently until the sauce thickens. Add salt and pepper to taste. Pour the sauce over the birds and decorate with watercress and orange slices.

Snipe

6

DUCK

Shooting season: Inland, 1 September – 31 January
Foreshore, 1 September – 20 February

Mallard, wigeon and teal are the species most likely to feature in the fowler's bag.

The drake mallard has a glossy green head, white neck ring and purple-brown chest. The rest of the plumage is mainly grey with a curly black tail. The duck has a speckled brown plumage. Both sexes have purple speculum bordered with white and bright orange legs. Like the pheasant, the mallard is surely familiar to everyone who has ever glanced at the village pond.

The cock wigeon is a medium-sized migratory duck with a rich chestnut head, grey finely striped back and flanks, a pink breast and white belly. The cock's white shoulder patches are clearly seen

Mallard

in flight. The hen is a duller, mottled brown with a white belly. Both sexes have pointed tails and a green speculum.

The teal is the smallest duck in the British Isles. The cock has a russet head with a cream stripe above the eye, grey finely striped back and flanks and speckled cream breast. The speculum of both sexes is green and black with a white border, otherwise the hen is a dull mottled brown. Both cock and hen have grey legs. These duck are to be found everywhere in the United Kingdom on rivers, lakes, ponds and marshes, and along the tidelines of muddy estuaries.

Wigeon

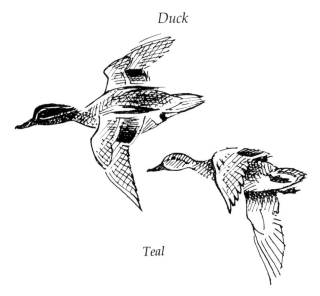

Duck

Teal

There are several species of wild duck but the mallard is the largest, probably the best known, and most frequently eaten. Then there are the smaller duck: wigeon, pintail, gadwall, shoveler, tufted, pochard and golden eye. Of these, the wigeon is most commonly eaten. The smallest and often the most highly acclaimed of the wild duck is the little teal which has a place of honour in the wildfowler's bag.

There is no doubt that the flavour of all duck is affected by their diet. Mallard feed on insects, earth-worms, potatoes, acorns and grain. Wigeon are grazing duck and feed mainly on a variety of grasses. Generally speaking, ducks which have been feeding on inland fields rather than coastal marshes are less strongly flavoured. Young September mallard fattened on grain from the stubble fields taste excellent and are best plainly roasted and served with an apple or orange sauce, sage and onion, or apricot and walnut stuffing.

One mallard will serve two people generously, but a wigeon is barely enough for two. Teal is the best flavoured of all the duck and just right for one person so it has the advantage that it may be cooked exactly to individual taste.

Wild duck do not need hanging as the fatty flesh tends to deteriorate rather than improve. There is no need to pluck the wings as there is so little meat on them. The flesh does not tear, but it may be necessary to remove any remaining down by rubbing the ball of the thumb over the skin. The skin crisps beautifully when roasted.

If you intend to use the duck in a casserole or pie, it is simpler to skin the bird, or just pluck the breast and legs and cut away the meat, discarding the rest of the carcass.

Many cookery books claim that wildfowl have little natural fat compared with the domestic duck and therefore need to be basted frequently to prevent the flesh from becoming dry. In fact, most duck, especially later in the season, have plenty of natural oily fat and are best roasted on a trivet, so that excess fat which has drained off during cooking may be poured off. This is especially important if wine, cider, fruit or vegetables are to be added during the cooking time. Drain off excess fat before adding the extra ingredients.

Duck is also good eaten cold, either carved thinly and served with beetroot, tomatoes or an orange salad, or the meat may be finely shredded and mixed with a light salad dressing and a variety of vegetables, fruit and nuts, with rice or pasta.

Duck may be successfully frozen, but for a shorter time than most other game: up to three months is ideal.

Mallard is sometimes available from larger supermarkets from mid-September to late January.

Roast Wild Duck   serves 4

Wild duck is best plainly roasted, but you may place a piece of orange, onion, apple or sage leaves inside the body cavity to add extra flavour. Remove these before carving the birds. Sage and onion, or apricot, walnut and orange stuffing (see p167) may also be served as an accompaniment. Many recipes for roasting wild duck suggest that they should be served slightly underdone to preserve the flavour. My family and I beg to differ and prefer them to be well done. This is, of course, a matter of individual taste, so if you prefer duck served rare, then reduce the recommended cooking time by about 20 minutes.

Brace of mallard or 3 wigeon	Salt
Optional: apple, orange, onion or sage	Watercress or sprigs of sage to garnish

Stuff the body cavities, with pieces of either apple, orange, onion or sage. Rub a little salt into the skin and place the duck breast down on a trivet in a roasting tin. Roast in a hot oven, 220°C (425°F), gas mark 7, allowing 1½ hours for mallard and 1 hour for wigeon. Turn the duck breast side up for the final 15 minutes of the cooking time to brown and crisp the skin.

If you wish to serve a stuffing with the duck, this may either be shaped into balls and placed around the duck on the trivet, or cooked separately on a greased baking sheet.

When cooked, keep the duck hot on a carving dish, remove the trivet and spoon off the excess fat.

Make a thin brown gravy from the pan juices.

Garnish the ducks with watercress or sage, and the stuffing if used, and serve the gravy separately.

Honey-glazed Mallard with Orange Sauce   serves 4

One of the culinary delights of early September is a brace of roast mallard which have been feeding on laid corn or stubble. These may be plainly roasted as in the previous recipe or, for a change, glazed with honey and served with a thin sauce made from orange juice and red wine.

Brace of September mallard
2tbsp clear honey
300ml (½pt) unsweetened
  pure orange juice
1 glass red wine

1tbsp cornflour
2 oranges
Salt and pepper
Watercress

Peel the oranges very thinly, using a potato peeler or sharp knife, and place the peel inside the body cavities of the mallard.

Place on a trivet in a roasting tin. Spread the honey over the breasts and legs, cover with foil and roast in a hot oven, 220°C (425°F), gas mark 7, for 1½ hours. Remove the foil for the final 15 minutes to allow the skin to become crisp and brown.

Remove the birds from the tin and keep hot on a serving dish. Remove the trivet and spoon off the excess fat from the tin.

Blend the cornflour with a little of the orange juice. Add the wine, the rest of the juice and the blended cornflour to the pan and bring to the boil, stirring all the time. Add a little salt and pepper to taste and pour into a sauce-boat.

Remove the pith from the oranges and cut into rings. Garnish the duck with the orange slices and watercress.

Serve with new potatoes, dwarf beans and the orange sauce.

Roast Teal   serves 1

Teal have a flavour too delicate to be masked by anything stronger than a little butter. The beauty of the teal is that as it is a perfect size for one person it may be cooked exactly to individual taste. This may be for as short a time as 20 minutes or as long as 40 minutes.

1 teal	Parsley and slices of lemon to
Melted butter	garnish

Brush the teal with the melted butter and place in a small roasting tin or shallow casserole. Cook in a hot oven, 220°C (425°F), gas mark 7, for 20-40 minutes according to taste.

Spoon the cooking juices over the bird and serve very hot garnished with parsley and slices of lemon.

Roast Mallard with Normandy Sauce   serves 4

This is another recipe ideal for September mallard and suitable for a special occasion. The traditional Normandy products of apples, fromage blanc and Calvados are used to make the sauce. Fromage blanc is a light, moist cheese with a creamy consistency similar to a thick-set yoghurt. It has the advantage of being lower in calories than cream, and yet has a softer and more delicate flavour than yoghurt. There are several brands now available from most supermarkets and specialist cheese shops.

Brace of September mallard	225g (8oz) fromage frais
350g (12oz) dessert apples,	2tbsp Calvados
peeled, cored and sliced	2tsp lemon juice
2-3 cloves	Watercress to garnish

Place the mallard breast down on a trivet in a roasting tin and cook for 1½ hours at 220°C (425°F), gas mark 7. Turn the birds over for the final 15 minutes to brown and crisp the skin.

To make the sauce, place the apples in a saucepan with a little water, cloves and lemon juice. Cook gently until soft, then liquidise or rub through a sieve.

Return the apple purée to the pan, add the Calvados and fromage frais and heat through, stirring continuously. Do not allow the sauce to boil.

Carve the duck onto a warm serving dish, pour over the sauce and decorate with watercress. *Bon appetit!*

Wild Duck with Sweet and Sour Pineapple Sauce serves 4

This tangy pineapple sauce goes well with the rich flavour of wild duck.

Brace of wild duck
8 pineapple slices canned in syrup
2tbsp white wine vinegar

1tbsp soy sauce
1 level tbsp cornflour

Roast the duck breast down on a trivet in a roasting tin in a hot oven, 220°C (425°F), gas mark 7, for 45 minutes.

Pour off any excess fat, remove the trivet and turn the duck breast side up. Drain the syrup from the canned pineapple rings and pour over the ducks. Return to the oven and cook for another 30-45 minutes. When cooked, place the duck on a carving dish and keep hot.

Blend the cornflour with the wine vinegar and soy sauce, then add to the cooking juices and stir over a gentle heat until it thickens and comes to the boil. Add a little salt if necessary.

Decorate the duck with the pineapple rings and spoon over a little of the sauce. Serve the rest separately.

Casserole of Wild Duck serves 4

This recipe uses the skinned legs and breast meat only. There is very little flesh on the rest of a duck, so it is ideal if you have limited time in which to prepare a meal for the family. If the duck has plenty of subcutaneous fat, this can easily be removed with the skin.

Brace of wild duck
150ml (¼pt) orange juice
150ml (¼pt) red wine or stock
Thinly pared rind and juice of
  1 orange

3 cloves
1tbsp flour
Bay leaf
Salt and pepper

Pluck the feathers from the legs and breast area of the duck. Cut off the large piece of meat either side of the breastbone, peel off the skin and fat and slice the meat thinly. Cut off the legs and skin them.

Place the flour in a saucepan, gradually blend in the orange juice and wine or stock and bring to the boil, stirring all the time.

Add the cloves, bay leaf, juice and thinly pared rind of the orange, salt and pepper, and finally the duck meat. Cover and simmer for about 1½ hours or until tender.

Serve with creamed potatoes and a green vegetable.

Wild Duck with Cider   serves 4-6

Early in the season, wild duck which have been feeding inland are usually lean and sweet tasting as they have not yet built up a surplus store of fat for the winter months. In this condition they are suitable for casseroling as an alternative to roasting. This recipe uses a dry cider together with tomatoes and young carrots which are usually still plentiful at this time of year.

2 lean wild duck   2tsp fresh or 1tsp dried sage
450g (1lb) tomatoes   600ml (1pt) dry cider
450g (1lb) carrots   Salt and pepper

Wild Duck with Cider

Pour boiling water over the tomatoes. Allow to cool and remove the skins. Chop the tomatoes roughly. Scrape and slice the carrots.

Place the vegetables in a large casserole, add the sage, salt and pepper.

Place the duck on the bed of vegetables and pour over the cider. Cook in a moderate oven, 180°C (350°F), gas mark 4, for 1½ hours.

Remove the duck from the casserole and cut the meat from the carcasses, leaving the legs whole. Put the meat back into the casserole and return to the oven for a further 15 minutes.

Serve with small new potatoes baked in their skins.

Duck and Pasta Salad   serves 4

Duck is equally good eaten cold and can be served with a variety of salads. If you are roasting duck for Sunday lunch, it is a good idea to cook an extra bird or two to serve cold the next day. Normally, a mallard will serve two people but, by finely shredding the meat and mixing it with other ingredients, it should stretch to four. Two cold wigeon will feed four people rather more generously.

Red and green peppers add colour to this salad and are cheap to buy in early autumn. Use wholewheat or verdi tagliatelle or ribbon pasta to add either extra fibre or colour. This salad is a complete meal and may be packed in individual containers for a picnic lunch.

Finely shredded meat from	225g (8oz) mushrooms, sliced
1 mallard or 2 wigeons	350g (12oz) cooked pasta
1 large red pepper, deseeded	6-8tbsp French dressing
and chopped	Parmesan cheese
1 large green pepper, deseeded	Chopped parsley to garnish
and chopped	

Toss the cooked pasta in half of the French dressing. Mix the meat, chopped peppers and sliced mushrooms in the remainder of the dressing.

Combine the pasta with the meat and vegetables and mix well. Sprinkle the Parmesan cheese over the salad and chill for ½ hour.

Sprinkle with chopped parsley just before serving.

Gill's Wigeon Pâté serves 6-8

This rich-flavoured rough-textured pâté is ideal to serve as part of a cold buffet table, as a starter to a meal, for picnics or shooting lunches. It is very easy to make, especially if you have a food processor.

6 wigeon breasts	1 clove garlic, crushed
225g (8oz) pig's liver	1 glass sherry
225g (8oz) minced belly pork	1 tbsp mixed herbs
225g (8oz) streaky bacon	Salt and pepper
1 small onion, chopped	Orange slices to garnish

Cut the rind off the bacon and remove any small bones or gristle. Stretch each rasher by pressing along its length with the back of a knife. Use the bacon to line the base and sides of a 900g (2lb) loaf tin.

Chop the liver, duck meat and onions using a food processor or knife, and add the minced belly pork, crushed garlic, herbs, sherry and seasoning, and mix well.

Spoon the mixture into the prepared loaf tin, taking care not to disturb the bacon rashers. Press the mixture down and fold over the overlapping bacon rashers.

Cover with the foil. Stand the pâté in a roasting tin and half fill with boiling water. Cook in a moderate oven, 180°C (350°F), gas mark 4, for 1¾-2 hours until the meat shrinks from the side of the tin.

Place another piece of foil over the pâté and top with weights. Leave to cool, then refrigerate overnight.

To serve, invert the tin onto a serving dish and decorate with slices of orange.

Gill's Wigeon Pâté. Step by step preparation guide

Spicy Duck Pie   serves 4-5

For a more unusual way of preparing duck, try this tasty duck and bacon pie flavoured with herbs and spices to provide a filling family meal for a winter's evening.

Breast meat and legs of
  2 wigeon or mallard
225g (8oz) lean bacon
2 large carrots
450ml (¾pt) chicken or
  game stock

1tbsp wholemeal flour
1tbsp mixed herbs
1 clove garlic, crushed
2tsp mixed spices
225g (8oz) shortcrust pastry
Beaten egg

Cut off the breast meat and legs from the duck and remove the skin. Chop the bacon and carrots.

In a saucepan, blend the flour with a little of the stock, gradually add the rest, stirring all the time, and bring to the boil.

Add the duck meat, bacon, carrots, herbs, garlic and spices and simmer for ¾ hour.

Place a funnel in a pie dish and add the duck, bacon and carrot mixture. Top up with the gravy. Cover with the pastry, make a small hole in the centre and decorate with leaves made from the pastry trimmings. Brush with beaten egg and cook in a hot oven, 220°C (425°F), gas mark 7 for about 40 minutes or until golden brown.

7

WILD GOOSE

Shooting season: Inland, 1 September – 31 January
Foreshore, 1 September – 20 February

(Left to right) Canada, pink-foot, greylag, white-front

Wild geese are found on the foreshores of Scottish coasts and The Wash, and on inland lakes, lochs and flat marshy estuaries.

The greylag goose is the ancestor of the domestic goose and is of a uniformly grey-brown colour. It has pink legs and a distinctive orange bill. It is the largest grey goose.

The pink-footed goose is smaller than the greylag and has a chocolate-brown head, plain brown breast, grey back and wings, pink legs and a pink and black bill.

The feral Canada is a very large grey-brown goose. It has a black head and neck with a distinctive white patch behind the eye. The back is dark brown with paler brown flanks and belly, a black bill, tail and legs.

The sale of wild geese is now prohibited by law, so few people have the opportunity to cook and eat these birds unless they have friends or family who are keen wildfowlers. By far the largest goose which may be shot in Britain is that native of North America, the Canada goose, introduced here as an ornamental bird to decorate the lakes of country estates, but now widely spread throughout lowland areas. The Canada provides good sport and is possibly the best flavoured of all the geese.

The smaller grey geese are the greylag, pink-footed and white-fronted. The latter is protected in Scotland. The pink-footed,

(Top) White-fronted and (below) pink-footed geese

whitefronted and most greylag geese are migrants, breeding in Iceland and other northerly outposts and arriving in Britain in early October. An increasing number of greylag geese breed here; migrant greylags generally arrive in late October.

It is a popular misconception that because geese live mainly on the foreshore they feed on, and therefore taste of, fish. This is far from the truth for no goose ever hatched has ever eaten a fish! Geese only roost on the estuaries and bays or large expanses of inland water, partly as a source of sand or grit which they need to aid digestion and partly for safety from foxes. They flight onto agricultural land each day from their roost in search of food. Their main diet consists of grass, but early in the season they will feed on grain on stubble fields and, later, pink-feet in particular will seek out mushy potatoes left behind after the crop has been lifted. Even later in the season they will look for winter wheat and feed on the young green shoots, often causing considerable damage to the crop.

The flesh of this muscular bird is dark and close-grained and has very little natural fat.

HANGING

As a general rule, geese are better if hung for at least two weeks to help to tenderise the meat. This is easy in wintry conditions and better if the geese have not spent too long in the back of a warm car. For geese shot in the early part of the season when the weather may be mild, hanging time may have to be reduced unless you have access to a cold store. As with other game, geese should be hung by the head, out of reach of predators, in a cool, airy place.

AGEING

Wild geese are difficult to age accurately, the more so as the season progresses. Generally, young birds have a flexible underbill and brightly coloured legs, and they lack the strong, clear-cut markings of the adult bird. Early in the season young geese have a V-shaped notch in the tail feather. After mid-November these guidelines begin to fail, so a good rule of thumb is, if in doubt treat the bird as an old one.

Geese are hard on the fingers to pluck, so it may be worthwhile

Wild Goose

Tail feather of a young goose showing 'V' shaped notch

paying a local butcher to do this. Cut off the head and feet and re-move the wings at the first joint. Draw in the usual way and wipe the bird clean. Truss as for pheasant, using a long skewer through the wings and upper body. Fold the neck skin underneath and try to catch this under a length of string looped around the ends of the skewer crossed over at the back and tied to the legs and parson's nose.

Geese may be frozen and stored for six to nine months, although I have cooked one which had been in the deep freeze for a year and it tasted excellent. Young birds are best roasted with a herb or fruit stuffing and served with a fruit jelly or sauce. The addition of a little liquid such as wine, cider, fruit juice or stock will help to keep the birds moist. It is a good idea to cook a goose breast down, covered with a lid or foil. The bird may be turned and the cover removed to-wards the end of the cooking time to allow the breast to crisp and brown. Older birds may be braised in a slow oven or made into pâté.

The weight of geese varies more than any other fowl or game bird. The average oven-ready weight of a Canada goose is about 2.7kg (6lb) and should serve six to eight people. The weight of grey geese may vary considerably from 1.3kg (3lb) for a young bird to as much as 4kg (8lb 12oz). The latter may be as old as twenty-five years and is sure to be a 'fork-bender'! On average, grey geese weigh 1.8kg (4lb) oven-ready and will serve four.

The following recipes are suitable for all species of geese. Adjust the cooking times according to the weight of the bird.

Roast Wild Goose serves 6-8

Roast goose of the domestic variety was the traditional Christmas dinner in many households before Dickens popularised the turkey. Wild goose, though not as succulent as its farmyard descendant, is equally full of flavour and, served with a savoury stuffing and a fruit jelly, makes a festive meal far better than a modern 'plastic' turkey at Christmas, or any time of the year for that matter.

1 young Canada goose	1tbsp flour
(2.7-3.6kg (6-8lb)), oven-ready	Sprigs of sage or parsley to
Sage and onion stuffing	garnish
300ml (½pt) stock	Quince jelly or apple sauce

Stuff the neck end of the goose with sage and onion, pull the neck skin under the body. Pass a skewer through the wings and upper body. Tie string around the ends of the skewer, catching the neck flap underneath if possible, cross the string over and tie around the legs and parson's nose. Place the goose breast down in a roasting tin and cover loosely with foil. Roast in a fairly hot oven, 200°C (400°F), gas mark 6, for 1½ hours.

Turn the goose over and baste with the stock. Cover and return to the oven for another 2 hours, basting occasionally. Remove the foil for the final 20 minutes of cooking time to brown and crisp the skin. Place the goose on a carving dish and keep hot.

Thicken the stock with the flour to make the gravy, seasoning if necessary.

Garnish the goose with bunches of herbs and serve with a selection of vegetables, gravy and quince jelly (see p163) or apple sauce.

Wild Goose with Cherries serves 4

The flavour of cherries and goose go well together. Add a little kirsch or brandy to the sauce and decorate with cherries and slices of lemon to make a colourful dish for a special occasion.

1 young goose (1.8kg (4lb)),	2tsp cornflour
oven-ready	Salt
1 can stoned red cherries	Lemon slices to garnish
2tbsp kirsch or brandy	

Truss the goose and rub a little salt into the breast. Stand in a roasting tin breast down, cover with a lid or foil and roast for 1 hour in a fairly hot oven, 200°C (400°F), gas mark 6.

Skim off any excess fat from the tin and turn the goose over. Drain the cherries from the can and baste the goose with the syrup. Return to the oven for 1-1¼ hours. Remove the lid or foil for the final 20 minutes and baste again.

Place the goose on a carving dish and keep hot.

Blend the cornflour with a little water, add to the cooking juices in the roasting tin and stir over a medium heat until the sauce thickens.

Add the kirsch or brandy and the cherries and heat through gently.

Spoon a little of the sauce over the goose, decorate the breast with lemon slices and place the cherries around the goose. Serve the rest of the sauce separately.

Leven Wild Goose with Orange Sauce   serves 4

The sharp tang of oranges goes well with all wildfowl and goose is no exception: add a dash of Cointreau or any orange liqueur to give the sauce extra flavour.

1 young goose (1.8kg (4lb)), oven-ready	300ml (½pt) pure orange juice
1 onion, chopped	2 small oranges
1 apple, cored and quartered	1 tbsp cornflour
1 orange, quartered	2 tbsp Cointreau
	Salt and pepper

Mix together the prepared onion, apple and orange and place in the body cavity. Tie the legs and parson's nose together with string, closing the body cavity as much as possible.

Place the goose breast down in a roasting tin. Cover with a lid or foil and cook in a fairly hot oven, 200°C (400°F), gas mark 6, for 1½ hours. Skim off any excess fat from the tin, turn the goose over and baste with 150ml (¼pt) of the orange juice. Roast uncovered for another 30 minutes.

Using a potato peeler, remove the rind from the oranges, cut into thin strips and blanch in boiling water for 5 minutes. Strain the rind.

Leven Wild Goose with Orange Sauce

Remove the pith from the two oranges and cut the fruit into rings with a serrated knife.

When the goose is cooked, place it on a carving dish and keep hot.

Blend the cornflour with the remaining orange juice and stir into the pan juices. Add the blanched orange rind, salt and pepper to taste and heat through gently until the sauce thickens. Finally, remove the pan from the heat and stir in the Cointreau.

Spoon a little of the sauce over the goose and decorate with the orange rings. Serve the rest of the sauce separately.

Casserole of Wild Goose   serves 4-6

This is a good way to deal with a bird of indeterminate age. The goose is first pot-roasted in a little stock, then carved and recooked with red wine and mushrooms. The second stage of cooking may be completed the next day.

1 wild goose
1 small onion
Thinly pared rind and
   juice of 1 orange
300ml (½pt) stock

300ml (½pt) red wine
100g (4oz) mushrooms, sliced
1tbsp flour
Sprig of thyme

85

Place the onion and orange rind inside the body cavity. Tie the legs and parson's nose together with string, closing the body cavity as much as possible.

Place the goose breast down in a flameproof casserole just large enough to take the bird. Add the stock and thyme. Cover and cook in a moderately hot oven, 190°C (375°F), gas mark 5, for 1½ hours.

Remove the goose from the casserole and allow it to cool.

Mix the flour with the orange juice and blend into the stock. Add the wine and bring to the boil, stirring all the time.

Remove the legs and wings, and carve the rest of the goose into small slices. Replace the meat in the casserole. Add the sliced mushrooms and cook at the same temperature for 1 hour.

Serve with jacket potatoes and spiced red cabbage (see p170-1).

Greygoose Pâté   serves 6

As the breast meat from a roast goose tends to be everyone's favourite portion, this pâté uses up the less popular meat from the legs and wings as well as the scraps from the carcass. Combine with the liver and minced pork to make a well-flavoured pâté to serve with salads and fresh bread.

225g (8oz) cooked goose meat	1tsp dried sage
225g (8oz) raw minced pork	1tsp mixed herbs
1 goose liver	150ml (¼pt) red wine
1 small onion	Salt and black pepper
1 clove garlic, crushed	Fresh sage to garnish

Chop the goose meat, onion and liver into very small pieces with a sharp knife or in a food processor using the metal blade. Combine with minced pork, garlic, herbs and seasoning and mix thoroughly.

To check the flavour at this stage, cook a little of the mixture in a frying pan, taste and add more herbs and seasoning if necessary.

Spoon the mixture into a well-greased loaf tin or earthenware casserole. Cover with foil, place in a roasting tin and half fill with boiling water. Bake in a moderate oven, 180°C (350°F), gas mark 4, for 1½-2 hours.

Remove the pâté from the water bath, cool and leave weighted overnight.

Turn out onto a serving dish and decorate with sprigs of sage.

Goose and Avocado Salad   serves 4

A small amount of cold roast goose may be added to a variety of salads to make a light lunch, a supper dish or a starter. Here, avocado pear and oranges are tossed in a light dressing and mixed with finely shredded goose meat.

275-350g (10-12oz) cold goose
   meat
1 large ripe avocado pear
2 large oranges

2tbsp olive oil
2tbsp lemon juice
Salt and black pepper

Peel the avocado pear, remove the stone and slice thinly. Place in a large serving bowl.

Using a sharp knife, peel off the skin and pith from the oranges. Hold over the serving bowl and cut out the segments of fruit, discarding skin and pips.

Combine the oil and lemon juice and pour over the avocado and oranges, mixing lightly.

Season the goose meat with salt and pepper and combine with the fruit mixture.

Serve with crusty bread or rolls.

Glazed Goose with Cider Apple Sauce   serves 4

Roast wild goose, basted with a spiced sugar glaze and served with a tangy cider and apple sauce.

1 wild goose (1.8kg (4lb)),
   oven-ready
450g (1lb) cooking apples,
   peeled, cored and sliced
300ml (½pt) dry cider

For the Garnish
Apple rings
Lemon juice
Oil

For the Glaze
2tbsp soft brown sugar
1tsp cinnamon
1tsp dry mustard
2tbsp cider (taken from the
   300ml (½pt))

Truss the goose and place breast down in a roasting tin or flame-proof casserole. Cover with foil or the casserole lid and cook in a fairly hot oven, 200°C (400°F), gas mark 6, for 1 hour. Spoon off any excess fat and turn the goose over.

Place the apples around the goose and pour the cider over the breast, reserving 2tbsp for the glaze. Cover and return to the oven for another 40 minutes.

To prepare the glaze, mix the sugar, mustard and cinnamon and blend together with 2tbsp cider. Remove the cover from the goose and baste thoroughly with the sugar glaze. Cook for a further 20 minutes or until the glaze is crisp. Transfer to a carving dish and keep very hot.

Stir the sauce to break up the apples to a soft purée and heat gently, allowing any excess liquid to boil away.

Dip the apple rings in lemon juice, brush with oil and grill lightly.

Decorate the breast of the goose with the apple rings and serve the sauce separately.

8

WOODPIGEON

No close shooting season

The woodpigeon is widespread throughout Great Britain except in the Highlands of Scotlands, the Outer Hebrides and the Shetland Islands. It is found chiefly in cultivated areas and woodland, but also in some urban areas. It roosts and nests in trees and hedges. Although by no means the most common British bird, it is by far the most destructive as it causes millions of pounds worth of crop damage each year.

In autumn and winter it feeds on grain from the stubble fields, clover, winter corn shoots, berries and frosted potatoes. Later, in very harsh, snowy conditions, the only available food may be kale, rape, cabbages or sprouts. Pigeons feeding on a diet of 'greens' will be in poor condition.

In spring and early summer they will feed voraciously on newly sown grain, peas, beans, maize or mustard, and are likely then to be in prime condition.

The woodpigeon has a broad white band across its wings and

after about two months old, white rings or patches on the side of the neck. The plumage is predominantly grey with a blue-grey head and paler flanks and underside. There is a purple and green gloss on the sides of the neck and the long tail has a black tip.

When shooting men talk about the pigeon they are really referring to the woodpigeon as other species, with the exception of the collared dove, are protected. The woodpigeon provides excellent sport and it has the advantage of being cheap and is usually available close to home where the shooter will have knowledge of locally grown crops. It is also increasingly in demand for the table with a thriving export trade in both fresh and frozen birds. It is becoming popular in this country and is more readily available from local butchers and supermarkets. In feather they are cheap to buy and will provide a variety of economical family meals, although they are considerably more expensive to buy oven-ready from the supermarket.

The pigeon is no newcomer to the British diet: as early as the sixteenth century large houses used to breed pigeons for food as well as for ornament and as messengers. Then they cost 10d a dozen. A century later the price rose drastically to 14s a dozen and two hundred years later they were still firm favourites at Victorian and Edwardian tables.

Although not strictly a game bird, the pigeon is one of the easiest and tastiest birds to prepare for the table and should never be neglected by the sporting wife, even though she may have a large number to deal with after a successful decoying expedition by someone in the family.

Freshly shot pigeon should not be left in a jumble in a game bag. Lay them out on a cold surface to allow them to cool naturally and gradually. Pigeons do not need to be hung, but if you are not able to prepare them immediately for cooking or the freezer it is best to empty the crops to prevent decomposing kale or other foodstuff from spoiling the flavour of the meat. Hang by the neck singly if possible in a cool, airy place. If you are dealing with unplucked pigeons in large numbers do not be daunted by the task of preparation, for they are the easiest of birds to pluck as the feathers can almost be rubbed off with your thumb.

Only young plump pigeons are worth roasting, in which case you need to pluck the whole bird, otherwise pluck only the breast and legs. The legs are worth keeping as they may be casseroled along with the 'steak' from the breast. If you have a large number of birds, the legs may be used for a pâté or terrine.

Having plucked the breast area and legs, cut off the legs with a sharp knife and remove the feet with scissors or secateurs. Lift up the base of the breastbone and cut up each side of the body until you come to the point where the wings are attached. Cut through the collarbones with the secateurs or strong scissors and remove

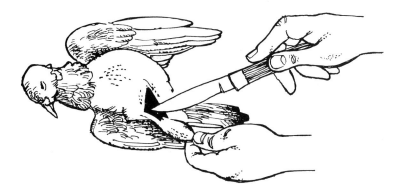

Having plucked the breast area and legs, cut off the legs with a sharp knife

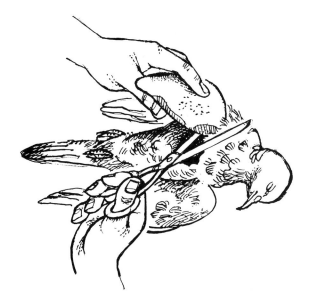

Cut through the collarbones with secateurs or strong scissors and remove the whole breast

the whole breast. Peel off the skin from the breast and legs. The liver may be kept for pâté or making stock, or cooked and fed to the dog along with the heart. If you have ferrets they will appreciate the rest of the bird, so nothing is wasted!

If the pigeons are to be cooked complete, then pluck the whole bird except for the wings as they have very little meat on them. Remove the head and feet with scissors or a sharp knife. From the neck end remove the windpipe and crop. Make an incision above the vent and draw out the intestines, liver and heart.

Pigeons will keep in a deep freeze for up to nine months. They may be frozen individually or in family-sized packs. A number of legs may be packed together for making pâté. The meat is firm and dense, and a whole bird will serve one person generously.

There are many ways to cook pigeon, either on its own or with other meat, vegetables, fruit and nuts. A young plump squab is delicious plainly roasted so long as it is covered to prevent it from drying out. Generally, the best results are achieved by long, slow cooking, in fact most dishes are improved if recooked the next day. In a pie they are best pre-cooked, ideally in a pressure cooker, to tenderise the meat.

According to their diet, pigeons are likely to be best flavoured during early autumn or spring.

Penrith Pigeons   serves 4

I am grateful to Mary Mason who kindly gave me this recipe when we visited her on our honeymoon. It was the first of countless pigeon dishes which I have cooked over the years.

The breasts and legs of 4
  pigeons
450g (1lb) carrots, diced
50g (2oz) raisins
25g (1oz) flour

For the Marinade
300ml (½pt) red wine
The juice of a lemon
6 cloves
Bouquet garni of parsley, thyme
  and a bay leaf
Salt and pepper

Place the pigeon breasts and legs in a bowl. Mix together all the ingredients of the marinade and pour over the pigeons. Leave in a cool place for 24 hours.

Place the pigeon meat in a casserole, thicken the marinade with the flour and pour over the meat. Add diced carrots and raisins and cook in a moderate oven, 180°C (350°F), gas mark 4, for 2 hours. Serve with rice and a green vegetable.

Stuffed Roast Squabs   serves 4

A squab is the name given to a young pigeon between four and six weeks old. They are delicious plainly roasted or with a savoury stuffing such as sausagemeat and mushroom.

4 squabs	50g (2 oz) mushrooms
8 rashers streaky bacon	25g (1oz) butter
	1tbsp lemon juice
For the Stuffing	1tbsp mixed herbs
225g (8oz) sausagemeat	Salt and pepper

Chop the mushrooms, place in a small saucepan with the butter and lemon juice and cook for 5 minutes. Allow to cool, then mix with the sausagemeat, herbs and seasoning.

Place the stuffing inside the pigeons. Truss the birds and lay two rashers of streaky bacon over each breast. Place in a small roasting tin and cook in a hot oven, 220°C (425°F), gas mark 7, for 40 minutes or until tender.

Serve the pigeons with redcurrant or cranberry jelly and gravy made from the pan juices.

Pigeon Pie   serves 4

Bacon and hard-boiled eggs are added to this pie to make a substantial meal. Allow one rasher of bacon and one egg for each pigeon breast. The meat is left on the bone for the first part of the cooking and then cut into slices before adding the pastry.

4 pigeon breasts	1 stock cube
4 rashers of bacon	Salt and pepper
4 hard-boiled eggs	25g (1oz) wholemeal flour
1 onion, finely chopped	225g (8oz) flaky pastry
1 clove garlic, crushed	1 egg yolk

Dissolve a stock cube in 300ml (½pt) hot water in a saucepan or flameproof casserole. Add the pigeon breasts, chopped onion, salt and pepper and simmer for 2 hours or until tender.

When cool, remove the pigeon breasts and cut the meat from the bone. Slice each half of the breast into three. Slice the bacon and hard-boiled eggs.

Place a funnel in a pie dish and put in layers of egg and bacon and pigeon meat. Thicken the stock with the flour and adjust the seasoning if necessary. Pour the gravy over the meat. Cover with flaky pastry, make a hole in the centre and glaze with beaten egg yolk. Bake in a hot oven, 220°C (425°F), gas mark 7, for 40 minutes or until the pastry is golden brown.

Squire's Pigeon   serves 4

In early spring the woods belonging to the local squire give pleasure twice over for our family. They provide excellent sport at roosting time as the pigeons return from feeding on the nearby fields and two days later they are on the table for supper. A few English walnuts stored from the previous autumn give bite and flavour to this casserole

Breasts and legs of 4 pigeons	1 small can tomatoes
1 tbsp soy sauce	1 red pepper, deseeded and
1 tbsp red wine vinegar	chopped
Juice of 2 large oranges or	1 onion, chopped
150ml (¼pt) pure orange juice	100g (4oz) button mushrooms
1 beef stock cube	50g (2oz) walnuts

Place the meat in a casserole. Mix together the orange juice, wine vinegar and soy sauce and pour over the pigeon meat. Cover and leave to marinate for 24 hours.

Dissolve the stock cube in 150ml (¼pt) boiling water and add to the casserole together with the chopped onion, red pepper and the tinned tomatoes. Cook in a moderate oven, 180°C (350°F), gas mark 4, for 2 hours.

Add the mushrooms and walnuts, seasoning if necessary, and continue to cook for a further 30 minutes.

Serve with baked potatoes, topped with sour cream, and Brussels sprouts.

Woodpigeon

Pot-roast Pigeon   serves 4

Pot-roasting in wine or stock is an alternative way to prepare whole pigeon. Lengthen the cooking time if you are not certain that the birds are young.

4 young pigeon	25g (1oz) split almonds, browned
8 rashers streaky bacon	in a little butter
1 large cooking apple, cored	Black pepper
and quartered	Watercress to garnish
150ml (¼pt) red wine	
1tbsp crab-apple or redcurrant jelly	

Place a quarter of apple inside each bird. Wrap each pigeon with two rashers of streaky bacon and place in a roasting tin or flame-proof casserole.

Pour over the red wine, cover with foil or a lid and bake in a moderate oven, 180°C (350°F), gas mark 4, for 1 hour. Remove the cover for the final 15 minutes to allow the bacon to brown.

Split the pigeon in half, trim away the backbone and arrange on a serving dish. Roll the bacon rashers and keep hot with the pigeons.

Add the redcurrant or crab-apple jelly (see p161-2) with a shake of black pepper to the pan and bring to the boil. Spoon a little of the gravy over the birds, serve the rest separately in a gravy-boat. Sprinkle the nuts over the pigeons, decorate with watercress and serve immediately.

Pigeons in Tomato Sauce   serves 4

This is a recipe which is usually popular with children, most of whom have a liking for tomato sauce. The flavour also goes well with pigeon.

Breast and legs of 4 pigeons	1tbsp tomato ketchup
100g (4oz) mushrooms, sliced	1 onion, finely chopped
400g (14oz) tin of tomatoes	

Place the mushrooms and onion in the base of a casserole. Lay the pigeon meat on top of the vegetables.

Purée the tinned tomatoes and combine with the tomato ketchup. Pour the tomato purée over the pigeons. Cover the casserole and cook in a moderate oven, 180°C (350°F), gas mark 4, for 2 hours.

Remove the breasts from the casserole and, when cool enough to handle, cut the meat from the breastbone into small slices. Return the meat to the casserole and cook for another 30 minutes.

Serve with baked beans and potato croquettes.

Pigeon and Mushroom Pie   serves 4

In early February, after the close of the game-shooting season, many farmers organise a 'pot a pigeon' day to deal with the vast numbers of marauding pigeons feeding on their crops. These birds are often more mature and need plenty of cooking. When preparing a pigeon pie it is a good idea to cook the meat on the bone to help enrich the gravy. The meat may then be taken off the bone before filling the pie dish.

6 pigeon breasts	Pinch of mace
100g (4oz) mushrooms, sliced	Salt and pepper
1 onion, finely chopped	1 tbsp cornflour
450ml (¾pt) chicken stock	225g (8oz) shortcrust pastry
6 cloves	Beaten egg
Bay leaf	

Place the pigeon breasts in a saucepan. Add the finely chopped onion, cloves, bay leaf and seasoning. Cover with the stock, bring to the boil, then simmer for 2 hours.

When cool enough to handle, remove the meat from the breast and cut each wedge into three.

Place a funnel in the centre of a pie dish and add the meat and sliced mushrooms.

Strain the bay leaf and cloves from the stock. Blend the cornflour in a little water or top of the milk and add to the stock, stirring all the time until the sauce thickens.

Adjust the seasoning if necessary, then pour over the meat and mushrooms. Cover with the pastry and decorate with the trimmings. Make a small hole in the centre and brush the pastry with beaten egg. Bake in a hot oven, 220°C (425°F), gas mark 7, for about 40 minutes or until the pastry is golden brown.

Serve with creamed potatoes and a green vegetable.

Cidered Pigeons   serves 4

A casserole of pigeons flavoured with cider, apples and spices, with a little cream added to make a delicious sauce.

The breast and legs of 4 pigeons	1tsp ground coriander
1 small onion stuck with 6 cloves	Salt and pepper
450g (1lb) dessert apples	3 tbsp top of the milk or
300ml (½pt) cider	single cream

Place the pigeon breasts and legs with the onion in a flameproof casserole. Pour over the cider and marinate for 24 hours.

The next day, peel, core and slice the apples and add to the casserole together with the ground coriander, salt and pepper. Simmer very gently for 2 hours.

Lift the meat from the casserole and allow to cool. Meanwhile, rub the apples through a sieve. Return the purée to the casserole, stir in the milk or cream and adjust the seasoning to taste.

Remove the meat from the breastbone and slice each wedge into three. Return the breast meat to the casserole and reheat gently for 15 minutes.

Serve straight from the casserole with creamed potatoes and minted peas.

Italian Pigeon   serves 4

This is a good way to cook an odd brace of pigeons which is not enough to make a meal on its own. Add minced beef and tomatoes to prepare an Italian-style sauce to which you can add spaghetti, noodles or any pasta that you like.

Breast meat from 2 pigeons,	1 small onion, chopped
finely chopped or minced	1tbsp mixed herbs
225g (8oz) minced beef	Salt and pepper
400g (14oz) tin of tomatoes	350g (12oz) pasta
1tbsp tomato purée	Parmesan cheese
1 clove garlic, crushed	

Mix the pigeon and minced beef together and fry with the onion and garlic until lightly browned.

Transfer to a saucepan and stir in the tinned tomatoes, tomato purée, herbs and seasoning. Simmer gently for 1½-2 hours.

Mix this sauce with cooked pasta of your choice and serve sprinkled with Parmesan cheese, coleslaw and a green salad.

Pigeon Pâté   serves 6

This pâté makes economical use of all those pigeon legs which tend to accumulate in the freezer left over from recipes requiring the breast meat only. Serve on crispbread or toast with celery, raw carrots and tomatoes for a snack or picnic meal.

Leg meat from 16 pigeons
  (about 225g (8oz) cooked meat)
225g (8oz) pork sausagemeat
150ml (¼pt) stock
1tsp mixed herbs
Salt and pepper

For the Marinade
150ml (¼pt) red wine
1 onion, finely chopped
2tsp mixed herbs
Bay leaf
Pinch of nutmeg

Place the pigeon legs in a small bowl. Mix together the ingredients for the marinade and pour over the meat. Cover and leave in the refrigerator for 2-3 days.

Put the pigeon legs, marinade and stock in a saucepan and simmer for 1 hour or pressure cook for 15 minutes.

When cool, remove the meat from the bones and pass through a mincer. Mix thoroughly with the sausagemeat, herbs, seasoning and enough of the strained stock to make a smooth moist mixture.

Place the pâté in a buttered ovenproof dish. Cover with a lid or foil and bake in a moderate oven, 180°C (350°F), gas mark 4, for 1½ hours. Chill the pâté overnight before serving.

Potted Pigeon   serves 4

Finely shredded pigeon meat is packed in individual moulds and set in jellied stock to serve either as a starter or as a light meal with salads and fresh bread.

Breast and legs of 4 pigeons
300ml (½pt) chicken stock
1tbsp mixed herbs
Bay leaf

½tsp grated nutmeg
Salt and pepper
25g (1oz) powdered gelatine
Parsley or watercress to garnish

Woodpigeon

Place all the ingredients except the gelatine in a saucepan and simmer for 1-2 hours or until the meat is very tender. Remove the pigeons and bay leaf.

When cool, remove all the meat from the bones and shred it finely.

Dissolve the gelatine in the stock.

Pack the meat loosely into wetted individual moulds—yoghurt pots or small margarine tubs are ideal. Pour over the jellied stock and leave in the refrigerator to set.

Turn out the moulds onto individual plates and decorate with parsley or watercress.

9

RABBIT

No close shooting season

One cannot envisage the countryside without the familiar sight of the rabbit for it is common throughout the British Isles.

The pelt of a rabbit has no less than three coats: a soft dense undercoat providing warmth and two outercoats giving a water-proof protection. The colour of the fur comes from these two outer coats and is predominantly grey-brown on the upper side, turning to reddish-brown at the back of the neck. The colouring is lighter underneath and the throat is white. The short fluffy tail, or scut, is brownish-black above and white underneath. The hind legs are much longer and stronger than the forelegs. The sexes are alike in colouring, but the male or buck may be slightly larger than the female or doe, with a shorter, thicker head and ears which may be torn from fighting.

The rabbit favours a moderate climate and inhabits heathland, sand dunes and fen country where the soil is soft for easy burrowing; it can also be found in woodland adjacent to open farmland where there is a good source of food. The rabbit feeds mainly on grass but can also cause severe damage to farm and garden crops and the bark of young saplings.

It is generally believed that the rabbit was introduced to this country by the Normans during the twelfth century when they were bred and protected in warrens. Some of the Norman conquerors arrived in England with warrener and his ferrets in tow. They were highly valued both for their meat and fur and frequently featured on the menu at impressive feasts such as coronations and enthronements of archbishops. The rabbit fetched a high price throughout the Middle Ages and in the seventeenth century they cost 8d a couple compared with only 4d for partridge.

The growing need for food in this country led to the gradual spread of warrens when land was set aside for the specific purpose of breeding rabbits, which, although confined by the boundaries of the warren, were otherwise quite wild. Landowners employed warreners to maintain the fences in a good state of repair to contain the rabbits and to keep out marauding foxes and poachers.

By the end of the nineteenth century rabbit warrens were becoming scarce owing to improved agricultural knowledge and techniques which made better use of the land through the cultivation of cereals and root crops. But the release of the rabbits was some farmers' downfall. One tenant farmer on a great estate was said to have committed suicide, saying: 'Rabbits have killed me.' They had fed on his crops and deprived him of his living. This was before the passing of the Ground Game Act in 1880 which gave tenants the right to kill rabbits on their land, thus giving some protection to their crops.

The additional source of food which the introduction of new crops gave to the rabbit, together with the growing interest in shooting for sport rather than just filling the larder, led to a startling growth in the rabbit population so that by 1953 it was estimated at between sixty and one hundred million.

Then in autumn 1953 came myxomatosis like the plague of the fourteenth century and in a matter of months the rabbit was almost eliminated, to such an extent that in some areas only one rabbit in two hundred survived. The disease had been known in some parts of the world for centuries and had been used in Australia in the 1950s to control the rabbit population. It is not certain how the virus reached England, but it was first reported in Kent in 1953 and from there it gradually spread until, a year after its arrival, there were over 250 outbreaks of the disease in 61 counties.

During the following thirty years numbers have steadily recovered as the rabbit has become virtually immune to the virus and a new generation has adapted to living above ground in small colonies where they are less vulnerable to the disease.

Today, the rabbit is almost as big a pest as ever, doing millions of pounds' worth of damage to farm crops, especially young corn, and even raiding garden produce. Landowners are legally required to control the rabbit population under the Pest Act of 1954. This is usually done by gassing, but there is talk of legalising the use of poisoned baits for controlling rabbits, a suggestion which many people view with alarm, and it would certainly not be well received by the great army of ferret owners should their traditional quarry and their sport be taken from them. A ferreted rabbit is highly prized as it is free from shot and therefore in clean condition. Much the same applies to a rabbit shot with a .22 rifle. The marksman aims for a head, neck or heart shot which result in clean kills and a minimum of damaged flesh. Rabbits peppered with shot-gun pellets, a mass of shattered bones and broken blood vessels are not popular in the kitchen and even the best cook cannot do justice to meat spoiled in such a way.

Imported rabbit meat is regaining popularity with the British public and is widely available both fresh and frozen from butchers' shops and supermarkets, although the wild rabbit has more flavour than those specially bred for the table.

PAUNCHING

Rabbits should be paunched as soon as they are cool. First 'thumb' the rabbit towards the vent to expel any urine from the bladder. A bladder punctured during paunching can cause the meat to become tainted. Using a sharp knife, cut the belly skin from vent to sternum and remove the intestines and stomach.

HANGING

In summer rabbits are best skinned the same day but in cooler weather they may be hung in a cool place by their hind legs for one to four days.

Rabbit

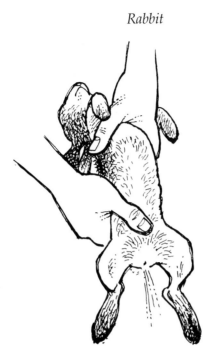

Thumb the rabbit towards the vent to expel any urine from the bladder

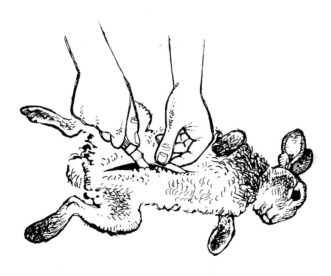

Paunching. Using a sharp knife cut the belly skin from vent to sternum

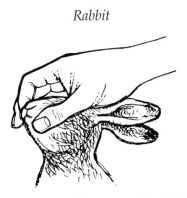

Ageing a rabbit. In a young rabbit, the lower jaw should yield to pressure between the thumb and first finger

AGEING

A young rabbit should be plump, with smooth fur, soft ears and smooth claws. The lower jaw should yield to pressure between the first finger and thumb. As a rabbit ages its ears become more leathery and the claws lengthen. A rabbit reaches adult size at four months and it then becomes more difficult to tell young from old. Some indication of a rabbit's age is how easy it is to skin. If the skin comes off easily and is inclined to tear, the rabbit is likely to be young.

SKINNING

Lay the rabbit on a worktop or table with its hind feet towards you. Start with the hindquarters by pulling the loose belly skin firmly towards you and peel it off around the tail and hind legs. Pull the legs

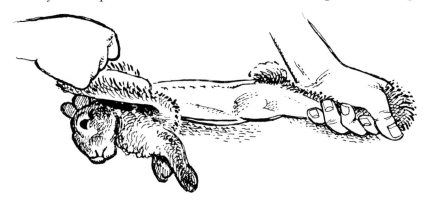

Skinning a rabbit

out of the skin. Cut off the feet with secateurs at the heel joint and remove the tail. Turn the rabbit around and work the skin up over the head pulling the front legs out. Cut off the front feet with secateurs and the head with a sharp knife. The head and complete skin may then be discarded.

Cut the diaphragm enclosing the heart and lungs inside the rib-cage. Keep the heart but discard the lungs. Remove and keep the kidneys and liver, which, together with the heart, may be used for stock. Wash the rabbit thoroughly in cold water, then leave to soak in cold salt water overnight. Rinse again in cold water before cooking or freezing.

Leave young rabbits whole for roasting. More mature rabbits should be jointed and used for stews, casseroles and pies.

JOINTING

Cut off the hind legs where they join the backbone and remove the front legs from the rib-cage. The back may then be cut into two or three joints. If you are preparing a number of rabbits for the freezer, keep back the top joint which includes the neck and rib-cage. There is very little meat on this joint and it is a minefield of tiny bones. Cook these separately and when cold strip the meat from the bones and use it in a game pie or pâté.

Young roast rabbit is improved with the addition of a savoury stuffing and covered with bacon to prevent the meat from becoming dry. A young rabbit cut into joints may be successfully cooked under the grill. As when roasting, to keep the flesh moist, either wrap a rasher of bacon round each joint, or alternatively, coat it in beaten egg and breadcrumbs. Older rabbits can be made more tender if marinated in wine, cider or beer before cooking. Virtually any chicken recipe will suit rabbit. One full-grown rabbit will serve four people. Rabbit may be stored for up to nine months in the deep freeze.

Roast Rabbit   serves 4

A young rabbit may be roasted with a savoury stuffing and plenty of fat bacon to keep the flesh moist. Sage and onion stuffing (see p166) goes well with rabbit, but you may like to try sausagemeat and apple, or apricot, walnut and orange (see p167) for a change.

1 young rabbit	1 tbsp sherry
8 rashers streaky bacon	Salt and pepper
Sage and onion stuffing	

Fill the body cavity of the rabbit with the sage and onion stuffing and sew the loose skin together.

Place in a roasting tin and season with salt and pepper. Lay the streaky bacon over the rabbit and cover the tin loosely with foil. Roast in a fairly hot oven, 200°C (400°F), gas mark 6, for 1 hour.

Remove the foil and bacon, baste well and return to the oven for a further 15 minutes. Roll the bacon rashers and return these to the oven to crisp.

Place the rabbit and bacon rolls on a serving dish and keep hot.

Add the sherry to the pan juices to make a thin gravy and serve the rabbit with roast potatoes, bread sauce and redcurrant or quince jelly (see p163).

Rabbit with White Wine Sauce   serves 4

Young rabbit joints are braised in stock with potatoes and parsley. White wine, yoghurt and mushrooms are added to make a delicately flavoured sauce which is thickened with the puréed potatoes.

1 young rabbit, jointed	150ml (¼pt) white wine
600ml (1pt) chicken stock	100g (4oz) button mushrooms
225g (8oz) potatoes, peeled and sliced	150g (5oz) natural yoghurt
1 tbsp freshly chopped parsley	Salt and pepper
1 clove garlic	Sprigs of fresh parsley and thyme to garnish

Crush the clove of garlic with a little salt in a saucepan. Add the rabbit joints, sliced potatoes, parsley, pepper and stock which may be made with a stock cube. Simmer for 1 hour.

Rub the potatoes through a sieve and return to the saucepan.

Add the button mushrooms, wine and yoghurt and heat gently for another 30 minutes. Adjust the seasoning if necessary.

Arrange the rabbit joints on a warm serving dish, pour over the sauce and decorate with sprigs of fresh parsley and thyme.

Sweet and Sour Rabbit   serves 8

Young rabbit joints are poached in a sweet and sour sauce. The meat is taken off the bone in fork-sized pieces and served with salads, rice or pasta to make an ideal dish for a buffet party. It may easily be prepared the previous day and reheated just before serving.

2 young rabbits, jointed	1 large onion, finely chopped
432g (15¼oz) pineapple pieces	1 tbsp soft brown sugar
in natural juice	2 tbsp white wine vinegar
6 large tomatoes, chopped	2 tbsp soy sauce
1 large green pepper,	Salt and pepper
deseeded and chopped	1 tbsp cornflour

Soak the rabbit joints in cold water for 24 hours, then rinse thoroughly.

Place all the ingredients, except the cornflour, in a large sauce-pan and simmer gently for 1 hour or until tender.

Allow the rabbit joints to cool, then remove the meat from the bones, breaking it into small pieces.

Mix the cornflour with a little water, blend into the sauce and bring to the boil, stirring all the time.

Return the rabbit meat to the sauce and reheat gently. Turn into a large warm shallow dish and serve with plain rice or pasta and a variety of salads.

Barbecued Rabbit

During the summer young rabbit joints may be successfully cooked on a barbecue as a change from chicken, sausages or burgers. Marinate the joints for 24 hours before cooking. Marinades usually contain an acid such as wine, wine vinegar or lemon juice to tenderise, oil or butter to add moisture and herbs or spices to give extra flavour. The joints should be basted frequently and turned with

Rabbit

tongs during cooking. Do not pierce with a fork or you will lose the natural juices. Both marinade and sauce are uncooked and are quick to prepare.

Young rabbit joints
  (allow 2-3 per serving)

Marinade
4tbsp oil
4tbsp wine vinegar
1 small onion, chopped
1tsp crushed rosemary
Salt and pepper

Barbecue Sauce
2tbsp tomato purée or ketchup
1tbsp red wine vinegar
1tbsp Worcestershire sauce
1tsp French mustard
1tbsp lemon juice
1tbsp brown sugar or honey

Place the rabbit joints in a shallow dish. Pour over the marinade and leave overnight in the refrigerator.

Oil the grill and heat for 30 minutes before starting to cook. Brush the joints with the marinade and grill for 10 minutes on each side, basting frequently with the marinade.

Brush with the barbecue sauce and continue cooking until the meat is golden brown.

Serve with the rest of the sauce, a plain green salad and some crusty bread.

Fricassée of Rabbit   serves 4

Joints of rabbit cooked in a creamy mushroom sauce is a popular dish in France. Rice makes a good accompaniment.

6-7 rabbit joints
Stock or water to cover the meat
1 large onion, sliced
225g (8oz) mushrooms
50g (2oz) flour
150ml (¼pt) single cream

Pinch of nutmeg
4 cloves
Bay leaf
Salt and pepper
Chopped parsley to garnish

Soak the rabbit joints in cold salt water for 2-3 hours or overnight. Rinse in cold water.

Place the joints in a saucepan with the sliced onion, bay leaf, cloves, nutmeg, salt and pepper. Add enough stock or water to just cover the meat. Cover and simmer for 1½ hours.

Strain off the stock which should be about 450ml (¾pt).

In a small saucepan, blend the flour with a little water. Gradually add the strained stock and stir until boiling, then stir in the cream.

Place the mushrooms in the saucepan with the rabbit and pour over the sauce. Heat through gently for 30 minutes.

Turn the fricassée onto a hot serving dish, sprinkle with chopped parsley and serve with boiled rice.

Hampshire Rabbit with Dumplings serves 4

This recipe revives childhood memories of returning home from school cold and hungry on a winter's evening to the welcoming sight and smell of rabbit and dumplings simmering on the Rayburn. In those days rabbit regularly provided a warm and filling family meal for country folk.

1 rabbit, jointed	4 cloves
1 chicken stock cube dissolved in 450ml (¾pt) boiling water	Salt and pepper
3tbsp wholemeal flour	*Dumplings*
225g (½lb) parsnips, sliced	100g (4oz) self-raising flour
225g (½lb) carrots, sliced	50g (2oz) shredded suet
225g (½lb) leeks, sliced	Salt and pepper
2 bay leaves	Cold water to mix

Blend the flour with a little cold water in a saucepan or flameproof casserole. Gradually add the chicken stock and bring to the boil, stirring all the time.

Add the rabbit joints, all of the prepared vegetables, cloves, bay leaves, salt and pepper. Cover with a well-fitting lid and simmer until the rabbit is tender. This may take 1½-2½ hours, depending on the age of the rabbit. Do not overcook or the meat will fall off the bones.

Mix the ingredients for the dumplings with just enough cold water to make a firm, stiff dough. Divide into four dumplings and add to the saucepan, replacing the lid carefully, and simmer for 20 minutes.

Serve at once with creamed potatoes.

Rescobie Rabbit   serves 4-6

This recipe is from Clare Graham, once proprietress of the highly rated Rescobie Hotel in Glenrothes. Bacon, onions and cider add a rich flavour to the gravy.

1 rabbit, jointed	2 tbsp flour
225g (8oz) streaky bacon	150ml (¼pt) dry cider
2 large onions, thinly sliced	300ml (½pt) chicken stock
75g (3oz) butter	1 bouquet garni

Chop the bacon and fry in butter with the onions. Brown the rabbit joints in the same fat and place in a casserole. Add the bouquet garni. Sprinkle the bacon and onion mixture on top.

Add the flour to the remaining fat and make a roux. Gradually add the cider and stock to make a gravy. Pour the gravy over the rabbit, cover the casserole and cook in a moderate oven, 180°C (350°F), gas mark 4, for 2 hours.

Serve with baked potatoes and a green vegetable.

Yorkshire Rabbit   serves 4

Marinating an older rabbit for a few days will help to tenderise the meat. Try a strong ale such as Theakston's Old Peculiar, a well-known Yorkshire brew, as a change from wine or cider.

1 rabbit, jointed	4 cloves
300ml (½pt) Theakston's Old	1 small tin tomatoes
Peculiar (or similar strong ale)	1 tbsp wholewheat flour
1 small onion, chopped	1 tsp dried basil
Crushed bay leaf	

Place the rabbit joints in a flameproof casserole. Add the onion, cloves, crushed bay leaf and ale. Leave for 2-3 days in a cool place.

Simmer on top of the stove for 2 hours.

Drain the tomatoes and add to the casserole.

Blend the flour with the tomato juice and stir into the casserole together with the basil. Continue to cook for another hour or until the rabbit is tender.

Poacher's Pie serves 4

Rabbit pie has been traditional country fare for many centuries. Any assortment of vegetables may be added together with some field mushrooms for extra flavour.

1 rabbit, jointed
1 onion, chopped
450g (1lb) mixed root vegetables, chopped
100g (4oz) field mushrooms, sliced
600ml (1pt) chicken stock
25g (1oz) wholemeal flour
Salt and pepper
225g (8oz) flaky pastry
Beaten egg

Blend the flour with the stock in a large saucepan and bring to the boil, stirring all the time. Add the rabbit joints, the chopped vegetables, salt and pepper. Cover and simmer for 1 hour.

Place a funnel in the centre of a pie dish and arrange the rabbit joints in the dish. Add the vegetables and gravy and cover with flaky pastry. Make a hole in the centre, decorate with the pastry trimmings and glaze with the beaten egg. Cook in a fairly hot oven, 200°C (400°F), gas mark 6, for 45 minutes.

Serve hot with potatoes and a green vegetable.

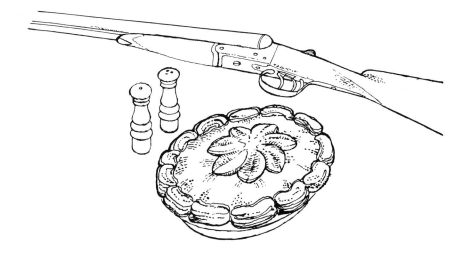

Poacher's Pie

West Country Rabbit serves 4

Cider and apples go well with all game meat and rabbit is no exception. The rabbit joints are cooked on a bed of apples. After cooking, yoghurt is added to the apple purée to make a smooth, creamy sauce.

1 rabbit, jointed	Bay leaf
675g (1½lb) cooking apples	150g (5oz) natural yoghurt
1 small onion stuck with 4 cloves	1tbsp sugar
300ml (½pt) dry cider	Parsley to garnish

Marinade the rabbit joints overnight in the cider together with the onion and bay leaf.

Peel, core and quarter the apples and place in a large saucepan. Lay the rabbit joints on top of the apples and pour the marinade over the rabbit. Bring to the boil and simmer gently for 1½-2 hours or until the rabbit is tender. Remove the joints from the saucepan and keep hot on a serving dish.

Strain the sauce, remove the onion and bay leaf and rub the apples through a sieve.

Pour the liquid and apple purée back into the saucepan, add the sugar and bring to the boil.

Stir in the yoghurt and heat gently for 5 minutes without boiling.

Pour the sauce over the rabbit and decorate with parsley.

Curried Rabbit serves 4

Curried dishes are best made with fresh rather than cooked meat, and as they require a long, slow cooking method to develop the flavour, this is a good way to prepare older rabbits.

6 rabbit joints	600ml (1pt) chicken stock
50g (2oz) butter	1tbsp mango chutney
1 small onion, chopped	1tbsp brown sugar
1 cooking apple, chopped	Juice of 1 lemon
4tbsp curry powder	Salt and pepper
1tbsp wholewheat flour	

Melt the butter in a flameproof casserole and add the onion and apple. Cook gently until soft.

Stir in the curry powder, then add the stock and bring to the boil. Add the rabbit joints, chutney, sugar, lemon juice and seasoning. Cover and cook in a moderate oven, 180°C (350°F), gas mark 4, for 2 hours or until the rabbit is tender.

Remove the rabbit joints and keep hot on a serving dish.

Blend the flour with a little cold water and stir into the curry sauce. Stir over the heat until the sauce has thickened.

Pour the sauce over the rabbit and serve with boiled rice, sliced tomatoes, banana and green pepper.

10

HARE

*No close shooting season, but hare may not be offered for sale
between 1 March and 31 July*

The two main species of hare found in the British Isles are the
brown or common hare and the blue or mountain hare.

The brown hare is considerably larger than the mountain hare
with much longer black-tipped ears and longer hind legs and is altogether less compact. The colour of the fur may vary from a soft
fawn to a sandy or reddish-brown which becomes greyer in the
winter months. The tail is white underneath and black on top.

The brown hare frequents mainly low land, favouring flat open
farmland and woodland, although it is found in some higher moorland areas. It lives in open country making for itself a form which is
a bed or seat hollowed from stubble, plough, grass or heather. The
brown hare feeds on grass and a variety of agricultural crops which
it frequently damages, or young saplings.

The mountain hare is similar to the brown but is finer boned and considerably smaller and stockier. It has long black-tipped ears and long hind legs. The fur is grey or reddish-brown in summer, but this usually turns white with a bluish hue in the winter, the ear-tips remaining black.

The mountain hare lives on the hills mainly in Scotland but also on moorland in parts of England. It feeds on grass and a variety of crops including heather and the bark and tops of young saplings. The mountain hare goes to ground more readily than the brown hare as its terrain has safe hiding and sheltering places, such as boulders or overhanging rocks, or it may go down into holes when the weather is bad or danger threatens.

Compared with a rabbit, a hare has a larger heart, greater volume of blood and longer legs as well as being considerably larger over-all, all of which contribute to its exceptional speed and powers of endurance. The other distinction is the hare's split lip, through which the teeth protrude in old age.

For centuries the hare has featured in the legends of great civili-sations. It is frequently linked with the moon and fire: in early Chinese mythology it was a symbol of resurrection. The hare is often depicted as hunted quarry in Roman, Greek and Egyptian art, and was thought to have mystical and supernatural powers.

The Hare Pie Scramble at Hallaton in Leicestershire re-enacts the ritual of scattering a sacrificial beast on the ground to promote fertility.

To the ancient Britons hares were sacred, but in the Middle Ages they were associated with witchcraft. Witches were said to trans-form themselves into hares, and the only way to kill a witch hare was, and still is, with a silver bullet.

The hare is a creature of unusual and fascinating habits and be-haviour, not least of which is its attempts to outpace a plane taxiing down a runway or its mad behaviour in the mating season which labels it moonstruck or the mad March hare.

It is assumed that hare was hunted for meat from very early times. If a countryman obtained a hare, often through poaching, he usually sold it to the gentry as it fetched more than a week's pay. Hare was not Hodge's liking as he found it had too much blood and the meat was too strongly flavoured for his taste. This was partly because he could not afford to cook it properly. The cost of prepar-ing a hare so that it was palatable was far beyond the means of ordinary country folk; they preferred the rabbit, far more simply prepared and not requiring extra expensive ingredients.

The old custom was to soak the hare in a quart of milk before cooking to make the meat paler and less strongly flavoured. Salt water or vinegar will do this equally well.

AGEING

A young hare or leveret has soft ears and a smooth coat. The teeth are small and white, the cleft or 'hare lip' is still quite narrow and the sharp claws are hidden beneath the fur. The coat of an adult hare becomes wavy and grey, white hairs may appear around the muzzle, and the ears are hard and dry. The teeth grow long and yellow with age, making the hare lip more pronounced. The claws grow long and become more rounded with wear and tear.

HANGING

In cold weather hares may be hung head down and unpaunched for up to a week.

SKINNING AND PAUNCHING

Unlike rabbit, a hare is skinned first and then paunched. This can be a messy job and it is wise to assemble everything you need close to hand before making a start. Wear an old apron or overall. You will need a large clean working surface, a very sharp knife, tough kitchen scissors, tin snips or secateurs, a bucket and plenty of newspaper to dispose of the entrails and skin. While skinning a hare try to keep the fur off the flesh.

Cut off the feet at the first joint using tin snips or secateurs.

With the head away from you, pinch up the belly skin and make an incision, taking care not to penetrate the body cavity.

Cut the skin around the back legs just below the tail. You can then work the skin off the hind legs.

Turn the hare around and draw the skin off the body and forelegs by pulling it towards the head.

Cut off the head and discard, together with the whole skin.

Using kitchen scissors or a sharp knife, cut from the fork between the legs up to the rib-cage.

Hare

Cut carefully through the paunch and draw out and discard the intestines. Keep the kidneys and liver, after carefully removing the gall-bladder.

Cut the diaphragm and draw out the pluck, discarding the lungs but retaining the heart, which may be used for stock.

At this point if you wish to keep the blood, pour any that has collected in the rib-cage into a small basin. The blood may be used in some recipes to enrich the sauce or gravy.

With a sharp knife remove the thin membrane which surrounds the meat.

JOINTING

Hare may be left whole for roasting or braising or it may be jointed according to your needs. For a saddle of hare remove all four legs and trim away any loose belly skin and the rib-cage so that the joint lies flat in a roasting tin or on a bed of vegetables. If the whole hare is to be jointed, divide the saddle into four or five even-sized joints. The front legs should be left whole, but the hind legs may be divided at the joint.

Wash the meat thoroughly in cold water and leave to soak in cold salted water for twenty-four hours, then rinse again thoroughly before cooking or freezing. This is a cheaper alternative to soaking in milk as described earlier. However, gourmets prefer the strong gamey flavour of hare, and they will cook it without the preliminary soaking. Likewise, the blood may be added in the final stages of cooking to further enrich the flavour. As in much game cookery, it is all a matter of taste.

Hare freezes well and will keep for up to nine months. It may be stored whole or divided into smaller packs, consisting of the saddle or legs only. If parts of the hare are badly damaged, label them accordingly and reserve for pies or pâté. Wrap any sharp bones with foil or greaseproof paper to prevent them from puncturing the freezer bag.

A fully grown hare will provide meat for six to eight people. A leveret should give four to six portions.

Older hares may be tenderised by marinating in beer, wine or cider for two to three days.

Hare

Roast Hare serves 4-6

Only young hares should be roasted. A stuffing will improve the flavour, and plenty of fat bacon laid on the hare will help to keep the flesh moist.

1 young hare
6 rashers streaky bacon
1tbsp flour
300ml (½pt) stock
1 glass red wine or port
Juice of ½ lemon

Forcemeat Stuffing
175g (6oz) fresh breadcrumbs

50g (2oz) shredded suet
1 egg, beaten
Juice and zest of ½ lemon
1tbsp chopped parsley
1tbsp thyme
2tsp marjoram
Salt and pepper
Lemon slices and watercress
  to garnish

Mix the dry ingredients for the forcemeat stuffing and bind together with the lemon juice and beaten egg. Stuff the hare and sew up the body cavity.

Place the hare in a roasting tin and completely cover with streaky bacon and then a layer of foil. Roast in a fairly hot oven, 200°C (400°F), gas mark 6, for 2 hours, basting every 30 minutes.

Remove the foil and bacon, baste well and return to the oven to brown. Remove the hare from the pan and keep hot on a serving dish.

Blend the flour with the pan juices, add the stock, lemon juice, wine or port and boil gently for 5 minutes.

Garnish the hare with slices of lemon, watercress and the bacon. Serve the gravy separately, with roast potatoes, a green vegetable and redcurrant or crab-apple jelly (see p161-2).

Saddle of Hare Moulin serves 3-4

A whole hare is often too large for a family meal. In this recipe the saddle is cooked in one piece on a bed of vegetables and herbs.

The saddle of a young hare
6 rashers streaky bacon
1 onion, chopped
1 large carrot, chopped
2 sticks celery, chopped
2 sprigs fresh rosemary

1 sprig thyme
Bay leaf
4tbsp single cream or top of
  the milk
Quince jelly

_118_

Remove the thin membrane covering the saddle and trim the rib-cage with scissors so that the joint may rest evenly in a shallow baking dish.

Place the chopped vegetables and herbs in the bottom of a shallow fireproof dish or baking tin. Lay the saddle of hare on top and cover with the streaky bacon rashers. Place buttered paper over the hare and cover with foil. Bake in a moderately hot oven, 180°C (350°F), gas mark 4, for 45 minutes.

Remove the foil and continue cooking for a further 10-15 minutes in order to crisp the bacon.

When the joint is cooked, carve in long thin slices lengthways and place on a hot serving dish with the bacon. Do not forget to carve the underfillet which has absorbed the flavours of the vegetables and herbs.

Strain the liquid from the baking dish and heat gently in a separate saucepan together with the cream or top of the milk, to make a light coffee-coloured sauce to pour over the sliced hare.

Serve with creamed potatoes, red cabbage, Brussels sprouts and quince jelly (see p163).

Hare Pâté   serves 8

Cooked hare meat is minced and blended with melted butter and lemon juice to give a smooth textured pâté. Serve as a first course with Melba toast or with bread rolls for a picnic lunch.

1 hare, jointed	Ground nutmeg
1 onion, sliced	100g (4oz) butter
1 bay leaf	1 tbsp sherry
Salt and 6 peppercorns	Black pepper
Grated rind and juice of 1 lemon	Fresh herbs to garnish

Soak the hare overnight in cold salt water.

Rinse thoroughly in cold water and place in a large saucepan with sliced onion, bay leaf, salt and peppercorns. Cover with water, bring to the boil and simmer gently for 3 hours or until the meat is tender. Leave to cool.

Remove the meat from the bones and pass through a mincer.

Melt the butter over a low heat and add the grated rind and juice of the lemon. Add to the minced hare together with the sherry and beat well with a wooden spoon. Add enough of the hare stock to make a firm mixture. Season with salt, black pepper and nutmeg.

Spoon the pâté into one large or several small soufflé dishes.

If you wish to keep the pâté for more than a few days, seal the top with melted butter and chill thoroughly. Decorate with fresh herbs just before serving.

March Hare   serves 4-6

Although you may not buy a hare in March, a book written in the early nineteenth century recommends leveret for eating at this time of year. Game books from large estates at this time showed that only young hares went to the table and that they were usually cooked in ale or rough cider and basted with a pint of cream. This recipe includes the cider but goes easy on the cream!

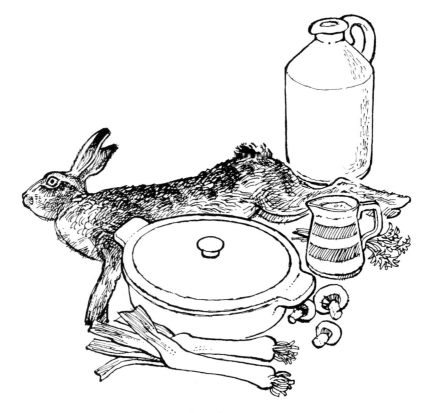

March Hare

1 young hare, jointed	1 tbsp cornflour
225g (8oz) bacon pieces, chopped	4 tbsp single cream
225g (8oz) button mushrooms	Freshly ground black pepper
2 leeks, chopped	Chopped parsley to garnish
450ml (¾pt) dry cider	

Place the hare joints, leeks and cider in a large casserole. Season with black pepper and leave to marinate for 24 hours.

Add the chopped bacon and mushrooms. Cover and cook in a moderate oven, 180°C (350°F), gas mark 4, for 2 hours. Transfer the hare and mushrooms to a serving dish and keep hot.

Blend the cornflour with a little water, stir into the sauce and bring to the boil. Simmer for 2 minutes. Stir in the cream and add more seasoning if necessary.

Pour the sauce over the hare and sprinkle with chopped parsley before serving.

Hare Pie   serves 6-8

Ox kidney adds extra richness to this hare and steak pie. Although this recipe uses the leg meat, any part of the hare is suitable.

4 hare legs	1 clove garlic, crushed
225g (8oz) stewing steak, diced	1 tbsp dried parsley
225g (8oz) ox kidney, diced	1 tsp dried thyme
100g (4oz) mushrooms, sliced	Salt and pepper
450ml (¾pt) beef stock	350g (12oz) flaky pastry
1 tbsp flour	Beaten egg

In a large saucepan blend the flour with 450ml (¾pt) beef stock. Add the hare legs, diced steak and kidney, sliced mushrooms, garlic, salt and pepper. Bring to the boil and simmer for 1½ hours.

When cool, remove the meat from the leg bones and slice into small pieces. Arrange the hare meat, steak, kidney and mushrooms in a pie dish with a funnel in the centre. Add the dried herbs and pour over the gravy.

Cover the pie with flaky pastry, decorate with the pastry trimmings and glaze with beaten egg. Cook in a hot oven, 220°C (425°F), gas mark 7, for about 40 minutes until well browned.

Hare Hotpot   serves 4

The leg joints of a hare are marinated in beer for 24 hours and then baked with vegetables and topped with sliced potatoes to make a complete meal for the family.

4 hare legs
300ml (½pt) beer
1 large onion, finely sliced
A few cloves
Sprig of dried rosemary
Pinch of ground coriander
900g (2lb) carrots, peeled and
  sliced

900g (2lb) potatoes, peeled and
  sliced
2 sticks celery, chopped
1 large tin tomatoes
300ml (½pt) stock
1 tbsp flour
Salt and pepper

Place the hare joints in a large casserole. Add the beer, onion, cloves and rosemary. Cover and leave to marinate for 24 hours.

Blend the flour with the stock and add to the casserole together with the carrots, celery, tomatoes, coriander, salt and pepper. Cover and bake in a moderate oven, 180°C (350°F), gas mark 4, for 1½ hours.

Add the sliced potatoes on top of the hare, season with salt and pepper, cover and return to the oven for another 1¼ hours.

Increase the oven temperature to 220°C (425°F), gas mark 7. Remove the lid from the casserole and bake for another 15 minutes to allow the potatoes to brown.

Saddle of Hare with Noodles   serves 3-4

Tender slices of hare are served with bacon-flavoured noodles and a rich sour cream and brandy sauce.

Saddle of a young hare
225g (8oz) streaky bacon
150ml (¼pt) sour cream
2 tbsp brandy

225g (8oz) noodles
Dried rosemary
Black pepper
Fresh rosemary to garnish

Using a sharp knife, remove the thin membrane covering the saddle.

Sprinkle the meat with dried rosemary and lay the bacon rashers across the back, completely covering the saddle. Place in a roasting tin, cover with foil and bake in the centre of a moderately hot oven,

Hare

190°C (375°F), gas mark 5, for 1 hour.

Cook the noodles in boiling salted water for 10 minutes.

Remove the bacon from the hare and chop finely. Mix with the noodles and season with plenty of black pepper.

Place the saddle on an ovenproof dish, cover with foil and keep hot.

Add the brandy and sour cream to the roasting tin and heat very gently.

Carve the saddle lengthways along the backbone in very thin slices, arrange in the centre of a long serving dish. Surround with the noodles, and pour the sauce over the hare. Garnish with sprigs of fresh rosemary and serve at once.

Jugged Hare   serves 6-8

In the past it was the custom to cook a hare in a jug or stew-jar in a moderate oven. If the oven became too hot the jug would either be placed in a baking tin surrounded by boiling water or stood in a saucepan of boiling water on top of the stove. Today, as few of us own a stew-jar, a good-sized earthenware crock is ideal for this classic dish.

1 hare, jointed	Crab-apple or redcurrant jelly
900ml (1½pt) beef stock	Parsley to garnish
made with a stock cube	
Zest and juice of 1 lemon	*Forcemeat Balls*
1 onion stuck with 4 cloves	100g (4oz) breadcrumbs
25g (1oz) flour	25g (1oz) shredded suet
150ml (¼pt) port	1tbsp chopped parsley
Sprig each of parsley and thyme	2 tsp chopped thyme
1 bay leaf	1 large egg, beaten
Salt and pepper	Salt and pepper

Soak the hare joints in cold salt water for 24 hours. Rinse thoroughly in cold water.

In a large casserole, blend the flour into the stock and slowly bring to the boil, stirring all the time.

Add half the port, hare joints, zest and juice of the lemon, onion, herbs and seasoning. Cover with a well-fitting lid. Cook in a moderately hot oven, 180°C (350°F), gas mark 4, for 2½ hours.

Add the rest of the port, adjust the seasoning if necessary, and

123

cook for a further 30 minutes.

For the forcemeat balls, mix together all the ingredients and form into eight balls. These can either be fried in shallow fat or baked in the oven for 1 hour.

Serve the hare straight from the casserole, decorated with fresh parsley, with the forcemeat balls and redcurrant jelly.

Harvest Hare   serves 2

Hares shot in early autumn will often turn out to be well grown leverets distinguished by their slim build. The fillets cut from the length of the saddle will provide a gourmet supper for two. Use the legs for a casserole.

Saddle of a young hare	2tbsp lemon juice
225g (8oz) mushrooms	2 cloves garlic, crushed
Oil for frying	Sprig of rosemary, parsley
	and thyme
For the Marinade	Salt and black pepper
4tbsp lemon juice	

Using a sharp knife remove the opaque skin from the saddle. Cut along the length of the saddle on one side of the back bone. Keep the knife close to the bone and remove the fillet in one long piece. Repeat on the other side. Carefully remove the two smaller underfillets.

Mix the ingredients for the marinade in a shallow dish. Coat the fillets in the marinade and leave to marinate for 8 hours turning the meat frequently.

Heat the oil in a large frying pan, add the mushrooms and the two large fillets and cook for 10 minutes.

Strain the marinade into the pan. Add the two smaller fillets and cook for a further 10 minutes, turning the meat from time to time.

Transfer the fillets to a hot serving dish, garnish with the mushrooms and pour over the pan juices. Serve with a green salad.

11

VENISON

Venison is the name given to the meat of any deer—roe, red, fallow and sika being the species most commonly available in Britain.

RED DEER

Shooting Season

	England	Scotland
Stag:	1 August–30 April	1 July–20 October
Hind:	1 November–28–9 February	21 October–15 February

The largest is the red deer, which is found mainly in the high hills and mountains of Scotland, in the forests of Cumbria and Norfolk and on moorland in South West England.

Venison

FALLOW DEER

Shooting Season

	England	Scotland
Buck:	1 August–30 April	1 August–30 April
Doe:	1 November–28–9 February	21 October–15 February

It is possible that the fallow deer was introduced to this country by the Romans. In the Domesday Book, thirty-one deer parks are recorded where fallow were kept securely in pens and used for food. Inevitably, some escaped and established themselves in forests and parks in both England and Scotland.

ROE DEER

Shooting Season

	England	Scotland
Buck:	1 April–31 October	1 April–20 October
Doe:	1 November–28–9 February	21 October–31 March

The roe deer may be found in woodland throughout Scotland and in most counties of southern England and East Anglia.

SIKA

Shooting Season

	England	Scotland
Stag:	1 August–30 April	1 July–20 October
Hind:	1 November–28–9 February	21 October–15 February

The sika was introduced to Britain during the latter part of the nineteenth century and is now well established in many counties of England and Scotland.

There is no close season for the tiny muntjac and Chinese water deer, but they are best stalked in winter when the foliage is at its minimum.

Unless you have an experienced stalker in the family you are unlikely to have to deal with a whole carcass, but if one does happen to come your way, it is wise to ask an expert, or pay your local butcher to skin and joint it for you. Venison is becoming more widely available to the general public owing to the promotion of deer farming on a commercial scale. Even so, a good proportion of red deer meat from Scotland is exported to Germany. Most game dealers are able to supply venison and many supermarkets have joints or stewing venison from autumn until spring, with the price comparing favourably with beef. Venison is darker in colour than beef and has the advantage of being very lean. Roe deer is considered to be the finest meat, followed by red and fallow deer. The flesh should be dark red and finely grained. A young beast is preferable to an older one as the meat is likely to be less strong and more tender.

HANGING

The length of time to hang a carcass must be governed by the season. The longer the beast hangs the stronger the flavour of the meat. A week to ten days is quite long enough in cool weather and in warm conditions four or five days will do.

The haunch and saddle are the joints for roasting or braising. Chops may be fried or grilled and the neck and shoulder used for casseroles or pies. The liver, often considered a delicacy in a young animal, is best eaten fresh. The underfillet, as in beef, is probably the finest cut of all and should be lightly grilled or fried. Treat a roasting joint as you would beef, except that, since it lacks natural fat, some should be added during cooking, but do not overcook, especially if you are leaving a joint to serve cold. The meat will shrink alarmingly, but there is virtually no wastage. It is by no means essential to marinate venison before cooking, but it does help to add moistness to the meat.

Venison freezes very well for at least ten months to a year as there is no fat to taint the meat. It will be less dry if marinated during thawing.

Roast Haunch of Venison   serves 8

As there is virtually no fat on venison, it will keep moist if it is covered with fat pork or streaky bacon and wrapped loosely in foil during cooking. It is not essential to marinate the joint first, especially if the animal is young, but it does add to the flavour and help to moisten the meat. Venison should be slightly undercooked, carved thinly and served very hot.

Haunch of venison	1 tbsp oil
8-10 rashers streaky bacon	1 tbsp red wine vinegar
Sprigs of rosemary	1 onion, chopped
Juice of 1 orange	Rind of 1 orange and 1 lemon
Redcurrant or elderberry jelly	6 peppercorns
Lemon slices to garnish	Bouquet garni

Marinade
300ml (½pt) red wine

Place the haunch in a large dish. Mix together the ingredients for the marinade and pour over the venison. Leave in a cool place for 2 days, turning and basting frequently.

Drain the venison and lay on a large sheet of foil. Sprinkle the meat with rosemary and cover with streaky bacon. Wrap the joint loosely, place in a large roasting tin and cook in a hot oven, 220°C (425°F), gas mark 7, for 15 minutes. Reduce the temperature to moderately hot, 190°C (375°F), gas mark 5, allowing 25 minutes per 450g (1lb). Open up the foil for the final 20 minutes.

Place the haunch on a carving dish, cover with foil and keep hot.

Strain the marinade and add to the pan juices together with the orange juice. Bring to the boil and adjust the seasoning.

Decorate the venison with lemon slices and serve with the gravy and redcurrant or elderberry jelly (see p162).

Venison Steaks   serves 4

The fillet or tenderloin is the prime cut and may be fried or grilled in the same way as beef steak. Before grilling, the steaks may be marinated for a few hours in oil and herbs, but this is not essential before frying. The important thing is not to overcook the steaks and to serve them immediately on hot plates.

Venison

4 venison steaks about 4cm (1½in) thick	225g (8oz) mushrooms
Butter or oil for frying	1tbsp dry sherry
Salt and black pepper	Chopped parsley to garnish

Heat the butter or oil in a large frying pan and lightly fry the mushrooms. Keep hot.

Sprinkle the steaks with a little salt and black pepper. Add the sherry to the pan and cook the steaks for about 5 minutes on each side.

Place the steaks onto hot plates and spoon a little of the pan juices over each steak. Sprinkle with mushrooms and chopped parsley and serve at once with a green salad.

Cold Venison with Chicory and Orange Salad   serves 4

Cold venison, slightly underdone and carved thinly, is excellent served with a fruit chutney, game chips and a coleslaw or waldorf salad (see pp169 and 170). If you are using the remains of a venison joint, cut the meat into thin strips and mix thoroughly with a dressed salad such as chicory and orange.

225g (8oz) cooked venison	Salt and freshly milled black pepper
4 medium-sized chicory heads	
2 large oranges	2tbsp chopped parsley or chives to garnish
4tbsp olive oil	
2tbsp orange juice	

Cut the venison into thin strips and place in a serving bowl.

Cut the chicory crossways into 5mm (¼in) slices and add to the bowl.

Remove the peel and pith from the oranges and cut into thin slices using a serrated knife. Add to the venison and chicory.

Put the oil, orange juice, salt and pepper into a screw-topped jar and shake until well blended. Pour over the salad and mix well.

Sprinkle with chopped parsley or chives and serve with new potatoes or fresh bread.

Venison and Tomato Cobbler serves 4-5

Any stewing venison or meat cut from the shoulder may be used for this popular family meal.

675g (1½lb) stewing venison, cubed	Black pepper
25g (1oz) seasoned flour	*Scone Mixture*
1tsp cinnamon	225g (8oz) self-raising flour
1 large onion, finely chopped	½ level tsp salt
300ml (½pt) beef stock	50g (2oz) margarine
225g (8oz) tomatoes, blanched, skinned and sliced	150ml (¼pt) cold milk
	Beaten egg
1tsp basil	Watercress to garnish

Coat the cubes of venison in flour seasoned with salt, pepper and cinnamon and place in a casserole.

Add the chopped onion, tomatoes, basil and black pepper and stir in the stock. Cover and cook in a moderate oven, 180°C (350°F), gas mark 4, for 2 hours or until the venison is tender.

To make the scones, sift the flour and salt into a mixing bowl and rub in the margarine until the mixture resembles fine crumbs. Add the milk and mix to a soft dough.

Turn onto a lightly floured board and knead quickly until

Venison and Tomato Cobbler

smooth. Roll out the dough to 5mm (¼in) in thickness. Cut into rounds with a 4cm (1½in) cutter.

Remove the casserole from the oven and increase the temperature to 220°C (425°F), gas mark 7. Uncover the casserole and top the meat with the scones. Brush with beaten egg and bake at the top of the oven for 20 minutes or until the scones are well risen and golden brown.

Decorate with watercress and serve with spiced red cabbage (see p170-1) or a green vegetable.

Veniburgers   serves 4

Visitors to the Game Fair in recent years may have lunched on hot dogs with a tasty venison sausage in the middle! Veniburgers are much easier to make at home and they should be popular with children. This is a good way to use up left-overs from a venison joint, but as the meat tends to be dry, add an equal quantity of minced streaky bacon.

225g (8oz) cooked venison	1 egg, beaten
225g (8oz) streaky bacon	Black pepper
1 small onion	Oil for frying
2tbsp breadcrumbs	

Mince the cooked venison, bacon and onion. Add the breadcrumbs and pepper and mix with the beaten egg.

Shape into four flat round cakes.

Fry in shallow oil until well browned on each side. Serve in baps with a dash of tomato sauce, English mustard or elderberry jelly (see p162).

Stalker's Breakfast   serves 4

After an early rising, the stalker will return home hungry for breakfast, and he might have a yearling in the bag. Whether or not he keeps the carcass, the liver is the stalker's perk, removed as soon as the deer is killed. It is considered a great delicacy as long as it is eaten really fresh. Serve with eggs, bacon and tomatoes as a breakfast treat for all the family.

Venison

1 venison liver from a young deer	4 tomatoes
4 rashers bacon	Triangles of toast
4 eggs	Butter or oil for frying

Wash the liver thoroughly under cold running water, then cut into thin slices about 5mm (¼in) thick. Heat some oil or butter in a frying pan and cook the liver for 5 minutes, turning once.

At the same time prepare the eggs, bacon and tomatoes in a separate pan so that you can serve the breakfast as soon as the liver is cooked.

Serve piping hot with triangles of toast and tea or coffee.

Braised Venison   serves 8

Venison marinated in wine and then braised on a bed of vegetables will help to keep the meat moist and succulent. If the joint has been frozen, allow it to thaw in the marinade so that all the juices are saved.

A haunch or saddle of venison	*Marinade*
300ml (½pt) stock	300ml (½pt) dry white wine
1 onion, chopped	1 tbsp oil
2 carrots, chopped	Zest and juice of 1 lemon
2 sticks celery, chopped	Bay leaf
1 tbsp rowan or redcurrant jelly	Sprigs of fresh parsley and thyme
Salt and pepper	to garnish
Parsley to garnish	

Mix together all the ingredients for the marinade. Place the joint of venison into a large dish and pour over the marinade. Leave for 2-3 days, turning and basting frequently.

Put the chopped onion, carrots and celery into a large casserole or baking dish, add the venison and pour over the stock and marinade. Cover with a well-fitting lid or foil and cook in a moderate oven, 160°C (325°F), gas mark 3, allowing 30 minutes per 450g (1lb). Remove the meat, carve and keep hot on a serving dish.

Strain the gravy into a saucepan and pass the remaining vegetables through a sieve or blender. Return the vegetable purée to the saucepan. Add the rowan (see p163) or redcurrant jelly and season to taste. Bring slowly to the boil.

Pour the sauce over the venison, decorate with sprigs of parsley and serve immediately with a selection of fresh vegetables.

Abbot's Venison

serves 6

Any cut of venison suitable for stewing may be used in this casserole. It is best cooked the day before it is needed, then reheated to improve the flavour and to ensure that the venison is tender.

900g (2lb) stewing venison, diced
6 rashers streaky bacon, chopped
300ml (½pt) Abbot Ale or
   similar strong ale
300ml (½pt) beef stock
1tbsp raspberry or red wine vinegar

1tsp brown sugar
1 clove garlic, crushed
1tbsp wholewheat flour
100g (4oz) mushrooms
Black pepper

Blend the flour with a little of the stock in a large flameproof casserole; gradually add the rest of the stock and ale, and bring to the boil, stirring until it thickens.

Add the raspberry or red wine vinegar, sugar, garlic, diced venison, chopped bacon and pepper. Cover and simmer very gently for 1½ hours.

The next day add the mushrooms and adjust the seasoning if necessary. Reheat in a moderate oven, 180°C (350°F), gas mark 4, for 1 hour.

Serve with jacket potatoes and sour cream.

12

SOUP AND GAME PIES

SOUP

The most important ingredient for any home-made soup is a good
well flavoured stock. As stock is made from vegetables and raw or
cooked bones, every time you prepare a game recipe you will have
the basis of a good soup.

Soup may be served as a first course or, with extra vegetables,
lentils, rice or pasta, it will make a main meal. Take soup in a
Thermos flask as part of a fishing or shooting lunch or serve as a
light meal or late-night snack. Soup may be served clear, or
thickened with vegetables puréed in a sieve, blender or food
processor, with cream and egg yolks. The thickness of soup is a
matter of choice and as soup is so versatile it is easy to adjust it to
your own taste.

Home-made soup and stock may be stored in a refrigerator for
two to three days but it should be brought to the boil each day.
Soup freezes well for two to three months but do not add cream,
egg yolk or starchy thickening until reheating.

All soups look even more appetising if they are garnished attractively. You may use anything that adds colour and texture, such as chopped chives or parsley, fried or toasted croûtons, grated cheese, or a swirl of cream or yoghurt.

Game Stock

Any assortment of game is suitable for making stock. Add seasonings and extra vegetables, rice or pulses to the prepared stock to make a variety of game soups.

2 pheasant or duck carcasses or 4 partridge carcasses	2 sticks of celery, chopped
1 large onion, peeled and quartered	2.25 litres (4pt) water
	6 peppercorns
	Bunch of parsley stalks

Place all the ingredients in a large saucepan. Bring slowly to the boil and simmer very gently for 3 hours.

Skim and strain the stock. Remove any scraps of meat from the carcasses and return these to the stock. Discard the bones.

The vegetables may be puréed and used to thicken the stock. For a clear game soup, season with salt and pepper and add a dash of sherry or port and a slice of lemon.

Cream of Game Soup   serves 4-6

A smooth creamy soup thickened with puréed vegetables and enriched with cream. Serve with fried croûtons of bread to give a crunchy contrast in texture to the smoothness of the soup.

2 game carcasses	Salt and pepper
2 carrots, sliced	2 tbsp single cream
1 large onion, chopped	Chopped parsley to garnish
2 sticks celery, chopped	
1.2 litres (2pt) water	*Croûtons*
2 bay leaves	8 slices stale bread
Mixed herbs	Oil and butter
Pinch of ground mace	

Break up the carcasses and place in a large saucepan. Add the water, chopped vegetables, bay leaves and herbs. Bring to the boil and simmer very gently for 2 hours.

Strain the soup and return the stock to the pan. Remove any pieces of meat from the carcasses and purée with the vegetables in a blender or vegetable mill. Discard the bones and bay leaves.

Stir the purée into the stock, add salt, pepper and ground mace to taste and slowly bring to the boil. Turn the heat down and stir in the cream.

Serve sprinkled with parsley and hand the croûtons separately.

Croûtons
Cut the bread into small cubes or triangles and fry in equal quantities of oil and butter until crisp and golden brown. Drain on kitchen paper.

Smoked Trout Soup   serves 4

A well-flavoured soup to serve as a first course or on its own for a filling snack.

225g (8oz) smoked trout fillet	600ml (1pt) milk
600ml (1pt) water	25g (1oz) cornflour
350g (12oz) potatoes,	4tbsp single cream
peeled and sliced	1tbsp lemon juice
3 medium-sized leeks,	Salt and black pepper
washed and sliced	Pinch ground mace
215g (7½oz) can tomatoes	Chopped parsley or dill to garnish

Place the fish in a saucepan and pour over 600ml (1pt) boiling water. Leave to stand for 15 minutes. Drain and flake the fish, reserving the water.

Add the potatoes and leeks to the saucepan with the reserved water and can of tomatoes. Bring to the boil and simmer for 20 minutes.

Purée the vegetables using a sieve or blender, then return to the saucepan.

Blend the cornflour with the milk, add to the saucepan and bring to the boil, stirring all the time. Reduce the heat and simmer for 3 minutes.

Stir in the flaked fish and season with salt, black pepper and ground mace. Stir in the cream and lemon juice.

Pour into a warm soup tureen, garnish with chopped parsley or dill, and serve with croûtons or crusty bread.

Stonesdale Grouse Soup   serves 4

Use the left-over carcasses and gravy from a pot-roast to make a
rich soup to serve as a first course or as a warming addition to a
picnic lunch.

2 grouse carcasses	Bay leaf
1 litre (1¾pt) gravy and water	4 peppercorns
1 carrot, chopped	1 glass of port
1 onion, chopped	1 tbsp cranberry jelly
1 small parsnip, chopped	Salt and pepper
2 stalks celery, chopped	2 tbsp single cream

Simmer the carcasses, chopped vegetables, bay leaf and peppercorns in the gravy and water for 2 hours.

Remove the bay leaf and the carcasses. Return any strips of meat
from the bones to the saucepan. Blend the vegetables or pass
through a sieve and return to the saucepan.

Add the port, cranberry jelly and seasoning if necessary and heat
through gently.

Pour into a warm tureen and streak with cream.

Pheasant Broth   serves 4-6

This soup makes good use of the carcasses left over from roast
birds. Served with wholemeal bread, it provides a substantial
meal.

2 pheasant carcasses	1 clove garlic, crushed
Left-over pheasant meat, diced	Bouquet garni
1.2 litres (2pt) water	50g (2oz) pearl barley
2 carrots, sliced	Salt and black pepper
2 stalks celery, chopped	Chopped chives to garnish

Place the carcasses in a large saucepan. Add the water and all the
ingredients except the diced meat. Bring to the boil and simmer
gently for 2 hours.

Remove the carcasses and strip off any remaining meat and put
back in the pan together with the diced meat. Discard the bouquet
garni. Adjust the seasoning if necessary and heat through for
5 minutes.

Decorate with chopped chives and serve with wholemeal bread.

GAME PIES

A traditional raised game pie is made with a hot-water crust pastry which is used to line a special game pie mould or cake tin, or moulded by hand into a pie shape. The pastry is filled with a mixture of raw or partially cooked game layered with various combinations of bacon, veal, minced pork, sausagemeat, livers or hard-boiled eggs. After the pie is cooked, a jellied stock is added to fill up the spaces and keep the pie moist.

Pies are a useful way to use up oddments of game; a badly shot bird, a tough grouse or partridge, a bag of rabbit rib-cages or pigeon legs. As well as a raised pie, the filling may be placed in a pie dish and covered with shortcrust, flaky or puff pastry and served hot or cold.

Pies with a potato or breadcrumb topping may also be served hot and make a change from pastry. Cold game pies and flans are ideal for picnics or a cold buffet meal and make an alternative to post-Christmas turkey meals. Serve with a variety of salads, chutney or pickles. Red cabbage or Brussels sprouts make a colourful accompaniment to hot pies.

Pies made with shortcrust, flaky or puff pastry may be frozen cooked or uncooked for up to two months. A hot-water crust pie does not freeze well as the pastry tends to crack and crumble after thawing. It will keep, however, for several days in the refrigerator.

Raised Game Fair Pie   serves 8

A pie made with a hot-water crust travels well and is ideal for a game fair lunch or a family picnic. Pack plenty of salads and some mustard or home-made chutney.

450g (1lb) cooked game meat, finely shredded
350g (12oz) pork sausagemeat
2 hard-boiled eggs, chopped
1 small onion, finely chopped
1tbsp mixed herbs
Salt and pepper
300ml (½pt) game stock (made from game carcasses)

3tsp powdered gelatine

Hot-water Crust Pastry
350g (12oz) plain flour, sifted and warmed
1 level tsp salt
75g (3oz) lard
150ml (¼pt) milk and water mixed
Beaten egg

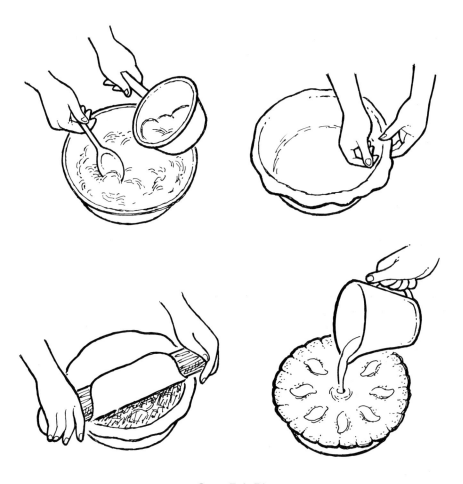

Game Fair Pie

From top left: Pouring the hot liquid into the flour; lining a cake tin with pastry; covering the pie; pouring the jellied stock into the cooked, cold pie

To make the pastry, put the lard, milk and water into a saucepan and heat slowly until the lard melts, then bring to a brisk boil.

Sift the flour and salt into a bowl. Make a well in the centre. Pour the hot liquid into the well, stirring all the time, and mix with a wooden spoon until the ingredients are well blended. Knead until smooth and crack-free.

Cut off a quarter of the pastry and leave covered in the bowl. Roll

139

out the remainder of the pastry into a circle and use to line an 18cm (7in) cake tin with a removable base or shape to line a 900g (2lb) loaf tin or special game pie mould.

Mix the sausagemeat, chopped eggs, herbs, onion and seasoning, and use half to line the base of the pie case.

Season the shredded game meat and add half to the pie. Then add the rest of the sausagemeat mixture and finish with the shredded game. Fill to within 2cm (¾in) of the top.

Roll out the rest of the pastry to make the lid. Seal well, then trim the edges. Decorate the top with the pastry trimmings and brush with beaten egg, reserving a little. Make a hole in the centre of the pie.

Bake in a fairly hot oven, 200°C (400°F), gas mark 6, for 30 minutes. Glaze again with beaten egg and reduce the temperature to moderate, 180°C (350°F), gas mark 4, for 1 hour. Allow the pie to cool.

Warm the stock and add the gelatine, stirring until dissolved. When cold and beginning to thicken, pour the jellied stock into the pie through a small funnel in the centre hole. It may be necessary to make a few small holes around the edge of the pie to add more stock.

Leave in a cool place overnight before removing from the tin.

Open Game Pie   serves 8

This game pie is made without a pastry top which makes it very much easier to fill the space between the meat and the pastry with a rich jellied stock. The top is decorated with black grapes and slices of orange making it a colourful centrepiece for a cold buffet table.

1 pheasant
2 pigeons, breast and legs only
225g (8oz) bacon pieces,
    derinded and chopped
225g (8oz) minced pork
2tsp mixed herbs
½tsp ground mace
300ml (½pt) game stock
Bay leaf
Peppercorns
3tsp powdered gelatine
Salt and pepper

Hot-water Crust Pastry
350g (12oz) plain flour,
    sifted and warmed
1 level tsp salt
75g (3oz) lard
150ml (¼pt) milk and water mixed

Topping
12 large black grapes
1 orange cut into 4 rings

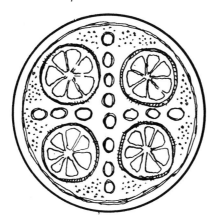

Open Game Pie

Cut off the breast meat from the pheasant and pigeons and cut into small pieces. Mix thoroughly with the chopped bacon and season lightly.

Remove the rest of the meat from the pheasant and the pigeon legs and either mince it or chop finely in a food processor. Combine with the minced pork, mixed herbs, mace, salt and pepper.

Place the bones in a saucepan together with a bay leaf and a few peppercorns, cover with water and boil for 1 hour to make a good stock. Strain the stock and reserve 300ml (½pt).

Lightly grease a 20cm (8in) cake tin with a removable base.

To make the pastry, sift the flour and salt into a bowl. Make a well in the centre.

Put the lard, water and milk into a saucepan. Heat slowly until the lard melts, then bring to a brisk boil. Pour into the well, stirring all the time and mix with a wooden spoon until well blended. Knead until smooth and crack-free. Roll out the pastry into a circle large enough to line the cake tin.

Place half of the minced-meat mixture into the pastry shell. Then add the breast meat and bacon mixture, followed by the rest of the minced meat. Crimp the rim of the pastry to make a decorative edge. Cover the pie with a double layer of foil. Bake in a fairly hot oven, 200°C (400°F), gas mark 6, for 30 minutes, then reduce the temperature to moderate, 180°C (350°F), gas mark 4, for 1½ hours. Remove the foil for the final minutes to allow the pastry edge to brown.

Leave the pie in the tin to cool.

Dissolve the gelatine in the warmed stock and allow to cool.

Cut the grapes in half and remove the pips. Slice the orange into rings and cut off the rind and pith. Decorate the top of the pie with the fruit.

Pour the jellied stock over the pie so that it seeps into the pie, filling the space between the meat and the pastry and embedding the fruit in a shiny layer.

Allow the pie to cool, and chill overnight before removing from the tin.

Serve with salads and chutney.

Christmas Pie   serves 4-6

A game pie using shortcrust pastry, which you are likely to be making anyway for mince pies, and has the advantage of being equally good hot or cold. Any combination of game may be used so search the freezer for half a hare or forgotten pigeon. Serve hot on Christmas Eve or give the cold turkey a rest on Boxing Day and serve cold with 'bubble and squeak', coleslaw and pickles.

900g (2lb) mixed game, jointed	Salt and pepper
350g (12oz) pork sausagemeat	225g (8oz) shortcrust pastry
1 glass red wine	1 beaten egg
300ml (½pt) stock	3tsp powdered gelatine

Put the jointed game in a saucepan with the wine, stock and seasoning and simmer for 2 hours. When cold, remove the meat from the bones and break into small pieces. Reserve the stock.

Use half the sausagemeat to line the base and sides of a 1.2 litre (2pt) pie dish. Add the cooked game, season lightly and top with the rest of the sausagemeat.

Cover the pie dish with the pastry, make a hole in the centre and decorate with the pastry trimmings. Brush the pastry with beaten egg and cook in a fairly hot oven, 200°C (400°F), gas mark 6, for 45 minutes or until the pastry is golden brown.

Dissolve the gelatine in 300ml (½pt) stock and gradually pour into the pie through a funnel in the centre hole.

Serve immediately hot, or leave until quite cold before slicing.

Game and Mushroom Flan   serves 4

An economical way to use up a small amount of left-over roast game, savoury flans make a satisfying lunch, supper or picnic meal and may be served hot or cold. The filling may be varied to suit whatever you have in the larder: hard-boiled eggs, sweetcorn or peppers may be used instead of or as well as the mushrooms; just add these ingredients to the basic white sauce together with the cooked game.

175g (6oz) cooked game meat, finely shredded
100g (4oz) mushrooms
1 small onion, finely chopped
25g (1oz) butter
Salt and pepper
20cm (8in) round cooked pastry case

Parsley to garnish

Basic White Sauce
25g (1oz) butter or margarine
25g (1oz) flour
300ml (½pt) milk

To make the white sauce, melt the butter in a saucepan and stir in the flour. Remove from the heat and slowly stir in the milk. Return to the heat, bring to the boil and cook for a few minutes, stirring continuously.

Slice the mushrooms and fry in butter with the chopped onion. Stir into the white sauce together with the shredded game. Season with salt and pepper and reheat for 2-3 minutes. Pour into the cooked pastry case and decorate with chopped parsley.

Game Pasties   serves 4

Serve hot with a mug of soup for a substantial snack. Serve cold with salads for a packed lunch or picnic.

225g (8oz) boneless game meat such as the breast of 1 pheasant or ½ rabbit
50g (2oz) streaky bacon
1 onion, grated
100g (4oz) potato, grated

225g (8oz) mushrooms, chopped
1tsp mixed herbs
Salt and pepper
350g (12oz) shortcrust pastry
Beaten egg

Make the pastry using 350g (12oz) flour and 175g (6oz) fat.

Chop the game meat and bacon into very small pieces. Mix

143

thoroughly with the vegetables, herbs and seasoning.

Divide the pastry into four and roll out into 20cm (8in) rounds using a plate as a guide.

Divide the filling between the four pastry rounds. Dampen the edges with cold water and draw up the edges to meet on top of the filling. Press firmly together and crimp to make a fluted edge. Place on a greased baking tray and brush with beaten egg. Bake in the centre of a hot oven, 220°C (425°F), gas mark 7, for 15 minutes, then reduce the temperature to 180°C (350°F), gas mark 4, for 1 hour.

Game Layer Pie   serves 4

Game, potatoes and tomatoes are layered and topped with grated cheese. Serve with a green salad for a midweek family meal.

2 rabbit joints and 2 pigeon breasts	Salt and pepper
1 onion, finely chopped	3tbsp tomato ketchup
1 carrot, sliced	450g (1lb) potatoes
1 parsnip, sliced	225g (8oz) tomatoes, sliced
450ml (¾pt) stock or water	50g (2oz) grated cheese
	Chopped chives to garnish

Place the game meat in a saucepan, add the chopped vegetables, seasoning, stock or water and simmer for 1½ hours. When cool, take the meat from the bones and slice into small pieces.

Liquidise the vegetables with some of the stock, return to the saucepan and blend with the remaining stock. Stir in the tomato ketchup.

Add the chopped game meat, mix together well and adjust the seasoning if necessary.

Peel and boil the potatoes for 10 minutes or until they are tender, but not soft, then slice thinly. Place a layer of potatoes in the bottom of a 1.2 litre (2pt) casserole. Add the meat mixture, then the sliced tomatoes and finish with a layer of potatoes. Cover and bake in a moderately hot oven, 190°C (375°F), gas mark 5, for 30 minutes. Uncover the pie and cook for a further 30 minutes or until the potatoes are brown and cooked through.

Sprinkle the grated cheese over the potatoes and return to the oven for 5 minutes.

Sprinkle with chopped chives and serve immediately with a green vegetable.

Quick Game Pie   serves 4

Another easy way to use up left-over portions of game and vegetables from a roast or casserole which are insufficient for a meal on
their own, but with the addition of bacon and mushrooms will
make an economical family meal. To keep the filling moist you
need a good 300ml (½pt) of stock or gravy, preferably thickened
with puréed vegetables for extra flavour.

225g (8oz) cooked game	300ml (½pt) gravy or thickened
100g (4oz) bacon	stock
100g (4oz) mushrooms	Black pepper
175g (6oz) fresh wholemeal	50g (2oz) butter or margarine
breadcrumbs	

Remove the rind from the bacon, fry lightly and cut into small
pieces.

Break the game into shreds and add to the bacon. Place in a 1.2
litre (2pt) casserole or pie dish.

Slice the mushrooms and add to the dish. Season with black pepper. Pour over the stock.

Melt the butter or margarine and mix with the breadcrumbs.
Sprinkle on top of the meat and mushrooms and bake in a moderate oven, 180°C (350°F), gas mark 4, for 1 hour.

Serve with plenty of fresh seasonal vegetables.

Instant Game Pie   serves 4

Convenient packet and canned ingredients are combined with left-
over cooked game to make an instant meal for busy school holidays
or to feed unexpected guests.

350g (12oz) cooked mixed game	50g (2oz) grated cheese
meat cut into small pieces	Sliced tomatoes to garnish
1 large packet instant potato	
275g (10oz) can condensed	
mushroom or chicken soup	

Mix together the condensed soup and game meat and place in a
1.2 litre (2pt) pie dish.

Make up the instant potato, spread over the game mixture and mark with a fork.

Sprinkle the grated cheese on top and decorate with slices of tomato.

Place on a baking tray and cook for 30 minutes in a hot oven, 220°C (425°F), gas mark 7, or until the pie is golden brown.

Serve piping hot with a can of peas and sweetcorn.

Vol-au-vent   makes 12

Small vol-au-vent cases filled with a savoury game and mushroom mixture may be served as a first course or as part of the menu for a buffet party. Cases may be made at home using puff pastry or bought uncooked, frozen or ready to use. The filling is quick to prepare and may be served hot or cold.

12 cooked vol-au-vent cases	225g (8oz) cooked diced pheasant
275g (10oz) can condensed	breast meat or rabbit
mushroom soup	

Place the soup in a saucepan; do not add any water. Add the diced game meat and heat gently.

Fill the pastry cases and put into a preheated moderate oven 180°C (350°F), gas mark 4, to warm through and crisp.

To serve cold, allow the mixture to cool completely before filling the vol-au-vent.

13

TROUT AND SALMON

Many shooting men and women are keen anglers. The timing of the seasons provides spring and summer fishing to match shooting in autumn and winter. The most commonly available game fish is the rainbow trout which is generally a dark grey-blue fish with a paler grey-blue belly, and characterised by the pinky-mauve band running from the jaw to the tail. Apart from the belly it is covered in fine black spots. The rainbow trout has been introduced to lakes, reservoirs, clear rivers and streams throughout the British Isles. It grows quickly and matures after two or three years and can weigh up to 4.5kg (10lb).

The native brown trout is to be found in most areas of the British Isles and with the rainbow trout is bred by trout farmers to stock lakes and reservoirs throughout the country. Generally, it is a

147

browny-green colour with a dark back and paler belly. It is dotted with black, red or orange spots on the head and body.

The sea trout is a beautiful fish coloured a silvery bluish-green, darker on the back and paler on the belly. There are black or dark-blue cloverleaf spots on the back and sides. It is found in most of the coastal waters of Britain and in cool unpolluted streams with direct access to the sea.

The salmon and sea trout are both migratory and go out to sea from the river of their birth when they are about eighteen months old. They return to their own rivers to spawn.

When at sea salmon have a blue back and silver sides with black spots and a pale belly. On returning to fresh water the fish turns brownish-green on its back with brownish-pink sides and black spots tinged with pink. This pink is lacking in the female.

Salmon and sea trout which have recently left their feeding ground at sea are in prime condition, full of natural oil, red flesh and silvery skin. This bright sheen gradually disappears as it swims upstream to spawn and the fish loses condition.

Any game fish will quickly deteriorate unless it is kept really fresh after being caught. Most trout are caught in the hot weather and if placed in a polythene bag on the river bank or at the bottom of a boat, will quickly become inedible. They will keep far better if wrapped in damp newspaper or a bass bag which allows the air to circulate, but best of all they should be placed in a cool bag or wrapped in newspaper and placed in an ice-box which many fishermen take for their beer and picnic. In this way the fish will reach home in perfect condition, at which time they should be gutted, cleaned and stored in the refrigerator or deep freeze.

Although there are no official close seasons for game fish, most water authorities restrict their seasons to spring until autumn. The summer months are undoubtedly the most popular for trout fishermen whereas the salmon fishing is at its best in the spring and autumn when the fish are running in fresh from the sea.

CLEANING FISH

Using a sharp knife, cut the fish open from the vent to the chin. With your thumb remove all the innards and cut away the gills. Using the tip of the knife, scrape away the blood from the backbone. Wash thoroughly in cold running water.

Cleaning fish. Using a sharp knife, cut the fish from the vent to the chin

BONING FISH

Clean the fish as above but remove the head and tail. Place the fish opened out flat, flesh side down on a table or work surface, and press firmly along the backbone with the fist or thumb to flatten it and loosen the bone. Turn the fish over and lift out the bone in one piece using the flat of the knife.

Boning fish. Press firmly along the backbone to flatten it and loosen the bone

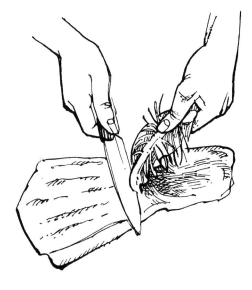

Boning fish. Turn the fish over and lift out the backbone in one piece using the flat of the knife

Filleting fish. Gradually slice the flesh away, working up the backbone

FILLETING FISH

Clean the fish and cut off the head. Make a cut across the fish just in front of the tail. Using a sharp knife with a flexible blade and keeping the blade flat, gradually slice the flesh away, working up the backbone until one side comes away whole. Turn the fish over and repeat on the other side.

Trout and salmon may be smoked either at home or professionally in a commercial smoke-house. The fish need not be in prime condition. Small home smokers may be bought cheaply enough and if you have a regular supply of fish, smoking makes an excellent alternative to the more usual cooking methods. For further useful information on home smoking consult Fred Taylor's excellent book *One For The Pot*.

FREEZING FISH

Ideally, all fish should be frozen the day it is caught. Trout and salmon are oily fish and may be stored for no more than two to four months. Smoked fish will keep for up to twelve months. Trout are usually frozen whole and should be gutted, cleaned and dried, wrapped in foil or polythene, sealed and labelled. Salmon may be frozen whole, cut into serving portions or 2.5cm (1in) steaks. Steaks may be frozen individually or packed with a double layer of cling film or wax paper between each portion.

Whole fish or large portions should be thawed out slowly. Steaks may be cooked partially frozen but the flavour is better if they are completely thawed before cooking.

CARVING FISH

A whole sea trout or salmon lying fully garnished on a large flat dish looks spectacular but needs careful carving if each portion is to be served in one piece and relatively free from bones.

Using a pair of fish servers, cut through the flesh from head to tail along the centre, following the line of the backbone, and remove the flesh from either side of this line to give about six small portions. Lift off the backbone and carve the underside in the same way. Try to remove any large bones from each portion and include a slice of lemon and a little of the garnish for each serving.

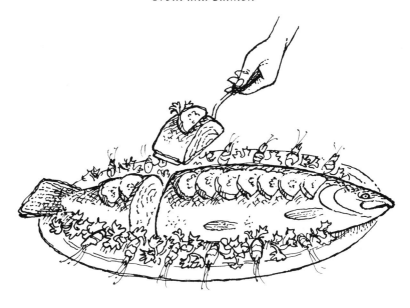

Carving a fish

TROUT

The flesh of trout caught from clean rivers and lakes will be pink owing to their diet of fresh water shrimps and other crustacea. Freshly caught trout have a delicate flavour and do not need elaborate cooking. There are many sauces which may be served with trout, but the fish is equally good plainly cooked with a little butter, lemon juice or herbs and served hot or cold with wholemeal bread and salad. It may be fried, grilled, poached or baked whole or filleted, or pâté or mousse may be made from fresh or smoked trout.

For those who do not fish, rainbow or brown trout may be bought from trout farms and are available from most fishmongers and many supermarkets. Trout is now cheaper than cod and is no longer the rich man's prerogative.

A large trout professionally smoked may easily be mistaken for salmon and, sliced thinly and served with a wedge of lemon and brown bread, it makes an ideal starter for a dinner party.

Small whole trout wrapped in foil may be successfully cooked on an open fire or barbecue.

152

Fried Trout   serves 4

Small trout freshly caught from the river need only the simplest of cooking to provide a superb family breakfast or supper. Make sure the plates are piping hot and serve the trout straight from the pan.

4 small fresh trout	1 tbsp oil
Seasoned flour	Juice of 1 lemon
50g (2oz) butter	

Roll the trout in seasoned flour.

Heat the butter and oil in a large frying pan but do not let it brown. Add the fish and cook over a moderate heat for about 5 minutes on each side or until golden brown.

Transfer the trout to hot plates; add the lemon juice to the butter in the frying pan and spoon a little over each fish. Serve at once.

Baked Stuffed Trout   serves 4

Baked trout with a savoury filling of mushrooms and apples make a substantial supper dish for the family. Serve hot with new potatoes and glazed carrots.

4 small trout	1 tbsp chopped thyme
100g (4oz) mushrooms	Salt and black pepper
2 dessert apples	Watercress and lemon wedges
1 tbsp chopped chives	to garnish
1 tbsp chopped parsley	

Split and bone the trout, removing the head but not the tail. Pat dry and lay flat.

Peel, core and dice the apples and chop the mushrooms. Mix together with the fresh chopped herbs.

Season the trout lightly with salt and black pepper and cover each fish with a quarter of the savoury filling. Roll up from head to tail.

Place the fish in a buttered casserole or flameproof dish which is just large enough to hold the fish. Cover with a lid or foil and bake in a moderate oven, 180°C (350°F), gas mark 4, for 40 minutes.

Decorate with watercress and lemon wedges and serve with the new potatoes and glazed carrots.

Trout with Almonds serves 4

A classic way to serve trout, the succulent texture of the fish contrasting with the crunchy fried almonds. This is a perfect dish for an informal lunch or supper party.

4 fresh trout	50g (2oz) flaked almonds
Seasoned flour	Fresh parsley and lemon wedges
50g (2oz) butter	to garnish
1 tbsp oil	

Roll the trout in the seasoned flour.

Melt the butter and oil in a large frying pan. Add the almonds and fry gently until brown. Remove from the pan, drain on kitchen paper and keep hot.

Add the trout to the pan and fry for about 5-8 minutes on each side until golden brown.

Place the fish on a hot serving dish, sprinkle with the almonds and garnish with fresh parsley and lemon wedges.

Trout with Almonds

Smoked Trout Salad   serves 4

Horseradish sauce, home-made for preference, is a classic accompaniment to smoked trout. Serve this colourful dish with a green salad and thin slices of wholemeal bread.

4 whole smoked trout	8 olives, pitted and halved
Mustard and cress	4 lemon wedges
4 large tomatoes, sliced	Horseradish sauce

Skin each trout and place on individual plates.

Decorate with mustard and cress, tomato slices, olives and a wedge of lemon.

Serve with a green salad, wholemeal bread and horseradish sauce (see p164).

Baked Sea Trout   serves 6

Sea trout is a smaller fish than salmon, slightly cheaper to buy and preferred by many for its delicate flavour and texture. Small fish, weighing about 450g (1lb), are ideal for frying or grilling and are known by various local names such as peal, sewin or herling. Although a good sea trout will weigh well into double figures, one of about 1.3kg (3lb) may be cooked whole to serve either hot or cold. It does not need a rich sauce to improve its flavour. Baking in foil is probably the nicest way to cook sea trout and salmon as the fish keeps moist and all the juices are preserved.

1 sea trout, 1.3kg (3lb)	Cucumber and lemon slices
Butter	to garnish

Gut, clean and dry the fish, but leave whole.

Measure out a large square of foil and spread with butter, making sure that the fish will not touch any part of the foil which is not buttered or it will stick.

Place the fish in the centre of the foil and fold to make a loose parcel sealed on top and at the ends. Place on a baking tray or in a large roasting tin and bake in a moderate oven, 160°C (325°F), gas mark 3, for 20 minutes per 450g (1lb). When cooked the eyes will have turned white.

To serve hot, leave the fish to stand in the foil for 10 minutes, then unwrap carefully, preserving the juices if you wish to make a sauce.

To serve cold, leave in the foil until quite cold, when it may be skinned and garnished with slices of cucumber and lemon.

Smoked Trout Pâté   serves 6

Smoked trout, curd cheese and yoghurt are blended together to make a low-calorie pâté. Serve with wholemeal toast and a tomato and fennel salad for a tasty snack meal.

225g (8oz) boned smoked trout	1tsp lemon juice
225g (8oz) curd cheese	Black pepper
Pinch of mace	Fennel or parsley sprigs to garnish
1tbsp yoghurt	

Remove the skin and any remaining small bones from the trout. Pound the flesh with the mace to a smooth paste.

Blend the curd cheese and yoghurt and season with black pepper and lemon juice. Mix thoroughly with the pounded trout.

Serve in an earthenware bowl or individual ramekins and decorate with the fennel or parsley.

This recipe may also be made with smoked salmon. Use up leftovers from a side or smoked salmon pieces which may be bought quite cheaply from delicatessens.

SALMON

Salmon is a rich, highly prized and highly priced fish, largely owing to its rarity. There is great anxiety about the future of the Atlantic salmon owing to high seas netting, abstraction, poaching and pollution. Many feel that the flavour may be over-rated and prefer the more humble herring. Indeed, if the herring were to become as rare as the salmon it would carry the label of exclusivity at present given to the salmon.

The best flavoured salmon are those caught in the spring or early autumn when they are running upstream from the sea. They should be bright-eyed, red gilled with shiny scales and the flesh should be firm and red. The presence of sea lice on salmon is a sure sign of their freshness.

Large portions or whole salmon are usually poached or baked in foil to serve hot or cold. Individual steaks or cutlets may be fried in hot butter or baked in wine, cream or wrapped in foil. Wafer-thin slices of smoked salmon, with lemon, black pepper and thin slices of brown bread, make a classic first course for a dinner party as does a spectacular salmon mousse.

Salmon Parcels   serves 4

Individual steaks are wrapped and sealed in foil parcels which retain all the juices and flavour of the salmon.

4 salmon steaks, 2.5cm (1in) thick	4 tbsp white wine
4 bay leaves	Salt and freshly ground pepper
4 sprigs of parsley	Watercress to garnish

Place each steak on a large square of buttered foil. Add a bay leaf, sprig of parsley, a little salt and black pepper.

Draw up the foil and, just before sealing, add 1 tbsp white wine to each parcel. Place the parcels in an ovenproof dish and bake in a moderate oven, 180°C (350°F), gas mark 4, for 15-20 minutes.

If the steaks are to be served cold, leave them to cool in the foil. Otherwise, unwrap the steaks and arrange on a serving dish. Discard the herbs, but pour the juices over the steaks.

Serve garnished with watercress.

Salmon Steaks with Soured Cream   serves 4

Simple to prepare, steaks baked in sour cream make a perfect supper dish for a special occasion.

4 salmon steaks, 2.5cm (1in) thick	Salt and freshly ground black
300ml (½pt) soured cream	pepper
	Chopped parsley

Place the steaks in an ovenproof dish. Season with salt and freshly ground black pepper.

Cover with the soured cream and bake in a moderate oven, 180°C (350°F), gas mark 4, for 25 minutes.

Sprinkle the salmon with chopped parsley and serve immediately.

Whole Poached Salmon   serves 12

The standard way of cooking a whole salmon is to poach it gently either in a fish kettle, which should have a trivet fitted with handles, or in a preserving pan, in which case a large fish may need to be curved to fit in. Salmon has such a delicate flavour that it is only necessary to poach it in lightly salted water flavoured with onion, carrot and herbs.

2.7kg (6lb) fresh salmon	1 tbsp salt
1 onion, sliced	Lettuce, cress, cucumber, wedges
1 large carrot, sliced	of tomato and lemon twists
2 bay leaves	for decoration
3-4 sprigs parsley	

Half fill the fish kettle or pan with water and add the sliced onion, carrot, herbs and salt. Bring to the boil and simmer for 30 minutes.

If using a kettle, place the fish on the trivet and lower into the water. Otherwise, use two long strips of muslin or foil wrapped around the fish, and, holding both ends, lower into the pan, curving to fit if necessary. Cover the pan and simmer very gently, making sure that the water does not boil, for 8 minutes per 450g (1lb).

Drain the fish and serve hot with Hollandaise sauce (see p164), new potatoes and salad.

To serve cold, allow the fish to cool in the liquid. Arrange on a large serving dish and decorate with twists of lemon, slices of cucumber and a mixed salad of lettuce, cress and tomatoes. Serve with mayonnaise. Alternatively, carefully remove the skin before decorating.

Cold Poached Salmon

This is a simple but foolproof method of cooking a piece of salmon of any size or a large whole trout which you intend to serve cold. Place the fish in a saucepan and cover with lightly salted water. Remove the fish and bring the water to the boil. Replace the fish and allow the water to come once more to the boil, then boil briskly for 2 minutes. Turn off the heat, cover with a tight-fitting lid and leave until quite cold, preferably overnight. The fish will continue to cook in the water as it cools, keeping the flesh moist. Drain well, decorate and serve with mayonnaise, new potatoes and salad.

Salmon Mousse   serves 6

Perfect as a first course or as part of a summer buffet party, salmon
mousse may be made in advance and frozen if necessary.

350g (12oz) cooked salmon,
   skinned and boned
300ml (½pt) milk
25g(1oz) butter
25g (1oz) flour
Bay leaf
4 peppercorns

1tbsp powdered gelatine
250g (9oz) fromage frais
2 egg whites, stiffly whisked
Salt and pepper
Sprigs of fennel and sliced
   cucumber to garnish

Place the milk in a saucepan, add the bay leaf and peppercorns,
cover and infuse over a low heat for 5 minutes. Strain and set aside.

Rinse the saucepan. Melt the butter and stir in the flour. Pour in
half the flavoured milk and blend with a wooden spoon. Add the
rest of the milk and stir until boiling. Boil for 2 minutes. Leave the
sauce to cool.

Dissolve the gelatine in 3tbsp warm water.

Flake the salmon into a bowl and mix well with the sauce. Season
with salt and pepper.

Add the dissolved gelatine. Fold in the fromage frais and stiffly
whisked egg white.

Turn into a lightly greased 1.2 litre (2pt) soufflé dish and leave in
the refrigerator to set.

Turn out the mousse and decorate with sprigs of fennel and
slices of cucumber.

Serve with crisp Melba toast.

Salmon mousse may also be served in individual ramekins
topped with a small sprig of fennel.

14

GOOD COMPANIONS

The following recipes are a selection of sauces, stuffings, jellies and salads as well as traditional accompaniments to serve with hot and cold dishes.

There are many fruits which may be harvested from the garden or hedgerow and with minimal cost made into fine jellies, sauces or chutney to accompany most types of game.

Although packet stuffings are convenient and quick to make, home-made varieties are far superior and you may ring the changes with alternative ingredients. Stuffings, like a game pie, may be different each time you make one according to what you have available.

There is an endless variety of winter and summer salads which add texture and colour to cold game, either served separately or mixed with finely shredded game meat.

Fried Breadcrumbs

Traditionally, either fried breadcrumbs or game chips are served with roast game.

8tbsp fresh white or brown   50g (2oz) butter
  breadcrumbs

Heat the butter on a low heat in a frying pan. Add the breadcrumbs and stir continuously until golden brown.
    Serve as a decoration to roast birds or on a separate dish.

Game Chips   serves 4

Although bought crisps or French fries are ideal to serve with game, it is possible to make your own as long as you prepare a few at a time and keep them moving in the hot oil to prevent them from sticking together.

450g (1lb) potatoes   Oil for deep frying

Peel the potatoes and cut into very thin slices. Soak in a large bowl of cold water for 1 hour. Drain and thoroughly dry the chips on a clean tea towel or kitchen paper.
    Fry in hot deep oil until golden brown, keeping the chips moving to prevent them from sticking.
    Drain well on crumpled kitchen paper and pile on a warm dish. Do not cover the chips or they will lose their crispness.

Crab-apple Jelly

A frequently neglected fruit of the hedgerow, crab-apples make a delicately flavoured jelly to serve with pheasant, partridge, duck or goose.

2.7kg (6lb) crab-apples   6 cloves
1.75 litres (3pt) water   Sugar

Wash the crab-apples and cut into quarters. There is no need to peel or core them. Put into a preserving pan, add the water and cloves. Bring to the boil and simmer for about 1½ hours.

Strain through a jelly bag or clean tea towel, preferably over-night. Do not squeeze the bag or the finished jelly will be cloudy.

Measure the extract and return it to the pan, adding 450g (1lb) sugar for each 600ml (1pt) extract.

Stir while the sugar dissolves and then boil briskly for about 10 minutes or until a 'jell' or setting point is reached. Test by putting a very little jelly on a cold plate and allow it to cool. The surface should wrinkle when a finger is pushed across the top of the jelly.

Skim with a slotted spoon and pour into clean warm jars. Cover with wax paper and a lid.

Elderberry Jelly

Gather the harvest of the hedgerows to make elderberry jelly, which is rich in flavour and colour, and especially good with grouse, venison and hare.

1.8kg (4lb) elderberries   Sugar
600ml (1pt) water

Wash the elderberries, place in a preserving pan and cook in the water until they are soft.

Strain the fruit through a jelly bag or a clean tea towel. Leave until the pulp has finished dripping, preferably overnight. Do not squeeze the bag or the finished jelly will be cloudy.

Measure the extract and return to the pan with 450g (1lb) sugar to each 600ml (1pt) extract.

Stir until the sugar has dissolved, then boil rapidly until a setting point is reached (see crab-apple jelly, above).

Remove any scum with a slotted spoon and pour into warm clean jars. Cover with wax paper and a lid.

Redcurrant or cranberry jelly may easily be made at home using the previous recipe for the elderberry jelly, substituting redcurrants or cranberries for the elderberries.

Use fresh redcurrants from the garden or 'pick your own' from a local soft fruit farm. Fresh cranberries are available in the shops during November and December.

Quince Jelly

This fragrant yellow pear-shaped fruit makes a fine jelly to serve with hare or goose.

1.3kg (3lb) quinces   Sugar
1.75 litres (3pt) water

Cut the quinces into quarters, but do not peel or core them, and place in a preserving pan with the water. Cover the pan and simmer very gently until the fruit is tender. Squash the fruit with a potato masher from time to time to make a soft pulp.

    Strain through a jelly bag or clean tea towel and leave overnight. Do not squeeze the bag or the finished jelly will be cloudy.

    Measure the extract and return to the pan with 450g (1lb) sugar for each 600ml (1pt) extract.

    Stir until the sugar dissolves, then boil rapidly for 10-15 minutes. Test on a cold plate for jelling. As soon as it sets, remove from the heat, skim, pour into warm clean jars and cover immediately.

Rowan Jelly

Although it may be a little sharp, rowan jelly makes a traditional accompaniment to venison and grouse and is also excellent with cold game.

1.3kg (3lb) rowanberries   1.2 litres (2pt) water
900g (2lb) eating apples   Sugar

Peel, quarter and core the apples and place in a large saucepan with 1.2 litres (2pt) water. Boil for 15–20 minutes or until the fruit is soft. Add the rowanberries and simmer to a pulp. Strain through a jelly bag or clean tea towel and leave overnight. Do not squeeze the bag or the jelly will be cloudy.

    Measure the extract and return to the saucepan. Add 450g (1lb) sugar to each 600ml (1pt) extract and boil for about 20 minutes or until a setting point is reached (see crab-apple jelly, p161-2).

    Skim with a slotted spoon and pour into clean warm jars. Cover with wax paper and a lid.

Bread Sauce

This is very easy to make and may be served with roast pheasant and partridge.

1 small onion stuck with 4 cloves	Salt and pepper
1 small bay leaf or 1 blade mace	Knob of butter or 1tbsp top
6tbsp fresh white breadcrumbs	of the milk
300ml (½pt) milk	

Place the onion, bay leaf or mace and milk in a saucepan on a very gentle heat, bring the milk slowly to the boil and then leave to cool.

Remove the onion and bay leaf or mace, add the breadcrumbs and seasoning and return to the heat, stirring until boiling.

Beat in the butter or top of the milk and serve hot.

Horseradish Sauce

The perfect accompaniment to smoked trout. To avoid tears when grating the horseradish, use a food processor or blender.

2tbsp grated horseradish	Salt and freshly ground black
150ml (¼pt) soured cream	pepper
1tsp icing sugar	

Blend all the ingredients together and chill for 2 hours before serving.

Blender Hollandaise Sauce

Serve with hot trout and salmon.

3 egg yolks	Salt and pepper
1tbsp lemon juice	75g (3oz) hot butter
1tbsp water	

Place the egg yolks, lemon juice, water, salt and pepper into a blender. Cover and blend for 5 seconds.

Pour the butter in a steady stream through the hole in the lid. Stop blending as soon as all the butter has been added.

Cranberry Sauce

Cranberry sauce may be served with any game bird, hare or venison, or added to a casserole.

150ml (¼pt) cold water
100g (4oz) sugar

225g (8oz) fresh cranberries, washed
1tbsp port

Place the water and sugar in a saucepan and heat gently to dissolve the sugar.

Add the cranberries and port and bring to the boil for 2-3 minutes, then simmer gently until the cranberries are reduced to a pulp.

Serve hot or cold.

Apple and Prune Sauce

A spicy sauce to serve with duck or goose.

50g (2oz) prunes
450g (1lb) cooking apples
4tbsp water

1tbsp sugar
½tsp cinnamon

Cover the prunes with water and leave to soak overnight. Next day, remove the stones and chop the fruit into quarters.

Peel, core and slice the apples. Place in a saucepan with the chopped prunes, cinnamon and water. Simmer gently until the fruit is soft. Add the sugar and stir until dissolved.

Pass the fruit through a sieve or blend to a purée. Serve hot or cold.

Mayonnaise   (makes 300ml (½pt))

Mayonnaise is the classic accompaniment to cold salmon and trout and although only a fraction cheaper to prepare at home, it has a better flavour than many bought varieties.

2 egg yolks
½tsp French mustard
Salt and freshly ground black
    pepper

300ml (½pt) corn oil, olive oil
    or a mixture of the two
1tbsp lemon juice or white
    wine vinegar

Put the egg yolks, mustard, salt and pepper into a bowl and beat with a small whisk or wooden spoon. Beat in 2tbsp oil very gradually, a drop at a time. Then stir in 1tsp lemon juice or vinegar.

Gradually beat in the remaining oil and, when thick and creamy, add the rest of the lemon juice or vinegar.

Transfer to a covered container and keep in the warmest part of the refrigerator for up to two weeks.

Should the mayonnaise curdle in the early stages, break a fresh egg yolk into a clean bowl and gradually beat in the curdled mixture a teaspoon at a time.

Green Mayonnaise

To 300ml (½pt) mayonnaise stir in:

2tbsp finely chopped parsley   1tbsp finely chopped chives
1tbsp finely chopped watercress

Orange Gravy

Serve with any roast game bird or wildfowl.

Rind and juice of 1 large orange   Salt and pepper
4tbsp port or red wine   1tbsp cranberry or redcurrant jelly

After roasting the birds, remove any excess fat from the pan juices. Add the orange rind and juice, port, salt and pepper and bring to the boil.

Remove the orange rind, stir in the jelly and heat gently.

Serve separately in a gravy-boat.

The following three stuffings are suitable for serving with duck and goose.

Sage and Onion Stuffing

225g (8oz) onions   1 small egg, beaten
100g (4oz) fresh breadcrumbs   Salt and black pepper
1tbsp chopped fresh sage or
  2tsp dried sage

Put the onions into a small saucepan, cover with water, bring to the boil and simmer until tender. Drain the onions and chop finely.

Combine the onions with the breadcrumbs, sage, salt and pepper, and bind together with the beaten egg.

Apricot, Walnut and Orange Stuffing

100g (4oz) dried apricots	1tsp finely grated orange rind
100g (4oz) fresh brown	Juice of 1 orange
breadcrumbs	1 egg, beaten
50g (2oz) chopped walnuts	Salt and black pepper

Soak the apricots overnight, then drain and cut into small pieces. Combine the breadcrumbs, walnuts, orange rind and seasoning and bind together with the orange juice and beaten egg.

Sausagemeat and Apple Stuffing

225g (8oz) pork sausagemeat	100g (4oz) fresh breadcrumbs
2 large cooking apples	Salt and pepper

Peel, core and finely chop the apples. Combine thoroughly with the rest of the ingredients.

Red Beet Salad   serves 4

Beetroot is known as red beet in the Fens to distinguish it from sugar-beet. Freshly cooked, it combines well with apples and cucumber to make a colourful accompaniment to cold grouse or partridge.

225g (8oz) cooked red beet	225g (8oz) cucumber
225g (8oz) eating apples	4tbsp oil and vinegar dressing

Skin the beetroot and cut into small dice. Peel the cucumber, cut into large slices and then dice. Peel, core and slice the apples.

Mix together with the dressing until the whole salad is a delicate shade of pink.

Apple Chutney   (makes about 3.6kg (8lb))

Excellent with cold game pie or spread on slices of cold game to make a moist filling for rolls or sandwiches.

2.7kg (6lb) cooking apples	1 level tbsp salt
900g (2lb) onions	1 level tsp pepper
1.2 litres (2pt) malt vinegar	1 level tsp ground ginger
675g (1½lb) soft brown sugar	1 level tsp mixed spice

Peel, core and chop the apples. Peel and chop the onions. Place in a large saucepan or preserving pan and add the salt, pepper, ginger, mixed spice and half the vinegar. Simmer until the ingredients are soft. Alternatively, pressure cook for 10 minutes.

Add the sugar and the remaining vinegar and stir until the sugar has dissolved. Continue to simmer until the mixture thickens, stirring occasionally.

Pour the chutney into clean warm jars while still hot. Cover with wax paper and seal with a lid.

Sloe and Apple Cheese

Sloes picked after the first frost will have softer skins. Any windfall apples may be used to make this cheese which goes well with any cold game.

1.3kg (3lb) windfall apples	300ml (½pt) water
900g (2lb) sloes	Sugar

Wash the apples and cut into quarters. Place in a large saucepan with the sloes and water and simmer until soft.

Press the fruit through a sieve and weigh the purée. Return purée to the pan and add 450g (1lb) sugar for each 450g (1lb) purée. Stir until the sugar dissolves.

Bring to the boil and simmer, stirring occasionally until the cheese is thick. This will take about 1 hour. Pour into clean warm jars and cover.

Watercress and Orange Salad   serves 4

Watercress and orange salad garnished with black olives is perfect to serve with hot or cold roast duck.

1 large bunch watercress	4tbsp olive oil
2 large oranges	1tbsp white wine vinegar
50g (2oz) black olives,	1tbsp lemon juice
stoned·and sliced	Salt and pepper

Wash the watercress, shake or spin dry and place in a polythene bag in the refrigerator for 1 hour.

Peel the oranges, discarding the skin and pith and slice into rings.

Put the olive oil, vinegar, lemon juice and seasoning into a screw-topped jar and shake until well blended.

Just before serving, arrange the watercress and orange slices in a salad bowl, pour over the dressing and garnish with the sliced olives.

Three winter salads with a crisp crunchy texture to serve with any cold game dish.

Red and White Slaw

100g (4oz) red cabbage	150ml (¼pt) mayonnaise or
100g (4oz) white cabbage	natural yoghurt
2 red eating apples	Salt and pepper
Lemon juice	

Shred the cabbage finely, discarding any tough outer leaves and the centre core. Place in a salad bowl.

Core the apples, slice thinly and toss in a little lemon juice to preserve the colour. Add to the cabbage.

Season the mayonnaise or yoghurt with a little salt and pepper, and mix thoroughly with the cabbage and apples.

Crunchy Nut Salad

225g (8oz) white cabbage,
    finely shredded
100g (4oz) grated carrot
1 small green pepper,
    deseeded and chopped

50g (2oz) dry roasted peanuts
50g (2oz) raisins
6tbsp oil and vinegar dressing

Thoroughly mix together the shredded cabbage, grated carrot, chopped pepper, nuts and raisins and toss in an oil and vinegar dressing.

Waldorf Salad

450g (1lb) firm red eating apples
1tbsp lemon juice
1tsp castor sugar
2tbsp natural yoghurt

2tbsp mayonnaise
4 stalks celery
50g (2oz) walnuts

Combine the lemon juice, sugar, mayonnaise and yoghurt.

Core and chop the apples and mix with the dressing. Leave for 30 minutes.

Slice the celery and chop the walnuts. Add to the apple mixture and mix thoroughly. Chill before serving

Spiced Red Cabbage   serves 4

A perfect accompaniment to any game dish, red cabbage needs to be cooked very slowly and is even better prepared in advance and reheated just before serving.

675g (1½lb) red cabbage
225g (8oz) cooking apples,
    peeled, cored and sliced
3tbsp red wine vinegar
3tbsp water
1tbsp soft brown sugar

3 cloves
½tsp ground cinnamon
½tsp ground nutmeg
Salt and pepper
1tbsp elderberry jelly

Wash the cabbage and cut into quarters. Remove the hard white stalk and shred the cabbage finely.

Place the cabbage in a large saucepan, add the sliced apples, sugar, vinegar, water, spices, salt and pepper. Cover with a well-fitting lid and cook over a low heat for 3 hours, stirring occasionally. Alternatively, cook in a large casserole in a moderate oven, 160°C (325°F), gas mark 3, for 2 hours.

Just before serving, add the elderberry jelly (see p162) and toss to glaze the cabbage.

Château Potatoes serves 4-6

New potatoes are fried golden brown and then baked in the oven until tender.

900g (2lb) small new potatoes	Salt and pepper
50g (2oz) butter	Chopped parsley to garnish

Scrape and dry the potatoes, and leave them whole.

Melt the butter in a flameproof casserole. Add the potatoes and cook over a moderate heat until golden brown all over.

Season with salt and pepper, cover the casserole and cook in a moderate oven, 180°C (350°F), gas mark 4, for 25-30 minutes.

Sprinkle with chopped parsley before serving.

Brussels Sprouts with Chestnuts serves 4

Complements any game dish; especially good at Christmas time when you are likely to have some fresh chestnuts and cooked ham in the larder.

450g (1lb) freshly cooked Brussels sprouts	50g (2oz) chopped ham
	25g (1oz) melted butter
225g (8oz) freshly cooked chestnuts	2tbsp top of the milk or stock
	Black pepper

Mix the cooked sprouts and chestnuts in a casserole.

Pour over the melted butter, top of the milk or stock and sprinkle with black pepper.

Reheat in the centre of a moderate oven 180°C (350°F), gas mark 4, for 20 minutes.

INDEX

Index

175